Religions of the World

by
F. H. M. Meade
A. W. Zimmermann
F. Whaling

Holmes McDougall Ltd., Edinburgh

ISBN 0 7157 2355-3

Printed and published by Holmes McDougall Ltd.,
Allander House, 137 Leith Walk, Edinburgh EH6 8NS.

Contents

Introduction

From earliest times most people have believed that there are forces in the world more powerful than themselves. They have believed that religion is real. Half a million years before Christ there is early evidence of religion in the ritual treatment of the skull of Peking Man and later skeleton finds. Further evidence of religion came in early man's desire to bury. Other evidence speaks to us from the walls of caves at places such as Lascaux in France where we have the early signs of religious art.

At many places around the world there remain tribes who often worship a remote high God and lower spirits or gods who are near at hand. This is often called primitive religion. Although we do not deal with these many primitive religions in this book, their roots reach back into the remote past of human history and provide further evidence of the fact that man is religious.

In this major revision of *Religions of the World* we look at most of the living religions. To assist us in so doing we begin with a framework of understanding that we hope will be helpful to the reader. All the religions treated in this book have a history and we look briefly at key events in those histories. All the major religions stress that there is a God or Reality behind the world. For Christians it is God as seen through Jesus. For Jews it is the one true God Yahweh. For Muslims it is the only God Allah. For Hindus it is Brahman. Buddhists deny that there is a God, but they have a goal Nirvana. Christianity, Judaism and Islam are called monotheistic religions because they believe in the worship of one God.

The major religions also emphasise a way that allows people to contact God or their goal. For Christians this way is Jesus, for Jews the Torah (Law), for Muslims the Koran, for Hindus normally a personal god, and for Buddhists normally the Buddha or his teaching, the Dharma.

All religions contain eight elements that we can look at more directly.

First they contain a religious community such as the Christian Church or the Buddhist Sangha that is often divided into different branches.

Second they contain rituals, sacraments and festivals whereby people can worship together.

Third they give a set of ethical values which say that murder, selfishness and evil are wrong.

Fourth they set up ways of social involvement which enable people to serve the world.

Fifth they stress certain scriptures which contain, among other things, important stories.

Sixth they emphasis certain beliefs about God or Reality and mankind.

Seventh they make these real at the popular level by religious aesthetic elements such as music, dance, sculptures, buildings and stained glass windows.

Eighth they enable people to experience God or Reality by prayers and spiritual helps.

In looking at these religions within this broad framework we will seek to understand them. What can be more important than that in this new global age in which we seek to create a new world for our children to inherit?

Christianity

JESUS AND THE BIBLE

Jesus and the Bible are two of the most important parts of Christianity. Jesus is more important than the Bible. Jesus of Nazareth is the most important thing of all. For two thousand years Christians have looked back to Jesus Christ as their example, their teacher, and their Lord.

Christianity includes a lot of things. It includes the churches that we see in our towns, the services that Christians go to, the good life they try to lead, the help Christians give to others, the Bible that they read, the beliefs that they hold, the hymns that they sing, and the prayers that they say. Behind all these is the figure of Jesus Christ and we begin with Him. Who was He, what do we know about Him?

Most of what we know about Jesus is to be found in the New Testament. This is the second part of the Bible. The first part of the Bible is the Old Testament which is also the scripture of the Jews.

Jesus was a Jew. He had a Jewish face, a Jewish figure, and a Jewish background. His first followers, who were called his disciples, were Jews. Jesus lived his life in the Jewish land of Palestine in the first century AD.

The first four books of the New Testament tell of the life of Jesus. The Christmas stories tell of his birth. The Easter stories tell us of his death. He also rose again from the dead in what is called the resurrection. This was the Good News that the early Christians passed on to others. Good News in Greek was Gospel. That is why these books are called Gospels. The story of how the early Christians preached the Good News to others is told in the rest of the New Testament.

The early Christians were Jews. Jews went to the synagogue every Saturday to sing and pray to God. When the Jews became Christians they still met every week to sing and pray to God. But they met on a Sunday. Sunday was the Christian Holy Day because it was on a Sunday that Jesus rose from the dead.

Through St. Stephen, St. Peter, St. John and Saul of Tarsus (who became St. Paul) the Gospel was taken from Palestine into other parts of the known world. Most of the New Testament was written in Greek. The early Christians used Greek and Roman ideas as well as Jewish ideas. They used the Greek word for God, theos, and our word theology is taken from it. Ever since, Christians have used words and ideas taken from their own culture to explain Jesus and the Bible to the people of their own time.

From a 12th century mosaic of Christ

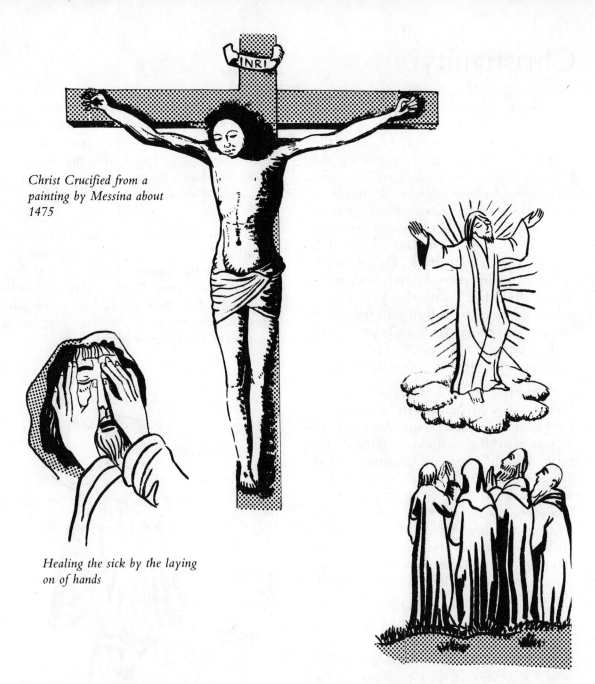

Christ Crucified from a painting by Messina about 1475

Healing the sick by the laying on of hands

The Ascension and the promise of the Holy Spirit

A baby wrapped in swaddling bands

Acts 1 3-9

After his resurrection, Jesus appeared to them and taught them about the kingdom of God . . . "You must wait," he said, "for the promise made by my Father, about which you have heard me speak; John as you know, baptised with water, and within the next few days you will be baptised with the Holy Spirit." When he had said this he was taken up, and a cloud received him out of their sight.

Christianity

At first the Christians often had to suffer for their faith. They were persecuted by the state. Jesus died on a cross and some of the early Christians also died at the orders of the Romans. The most famous of the early persecutions came in AD 64 at the hands of Nero. He is said to have started a fire in Rome, and then to have blamed it on the Christians. The Christians who died became known as martyrs. Their bravery had an effect on others. Martyrs such as St. Alban gave their names to well-known towns. In the midst of their pain they were known to cry out, 'I am a Christian, and with us no evil finds a place'. The death of the martyrs led to the growth of the church.

In the year AD 312 a Roman emperor became a Christian. His name was Constantine. The story is told that in AD 312 he was marching to Rome to fight a hard battle. He called upon the Christian God to help him in the battle. He promised that if he won the battle he would become a Christian. It is said that he saw the sign of a cross in the sky and on the cross were written the words, 'By this sign you shall conquer'. Constantine won the battle and from then on he helped the Christian church.

He called a famous council of bishops to Nicaea in AD 325. They agreed on the words of the Nicene Creed. This summed up the agreed teachings of the Christians, and is still said in some churches by Christians today.

By the time of Constantine, the small and weak church of St. Paul and St. Peter had grown in strength. Many people had become Christians in the Roman Empire. They were admired because they died bravely. They lived good lives. They were honest and good citizens. Their leaders were respected. The Christians were well organised by their deacons, priests and bishops. They knew what they believed and had worked out some of the main points in their teachings. The Christians said that God loved all persons. They were ready to take the Good News of God's love to others.

Up to the time of Constantine, the Christian Church had spread because the Christians had good news to tell and they told it with vigour. By the end of the fourth century, Christianity had become the official religion of the Roman Empire. It spread as the religion of the state.

The death of St. Alban

8

The Roman Empire at the time of Constantine

Constantine built this arch in Rome to celebrate his victory and his becoming a Christian.

In the early Church some symbols of Christ were:
a fish–the initial letters of Jesus Christ God's Son Saviour make the Greek word for fish
a lamb–to show Jesus sacrificed himself for us
XP–These are the first two sounds of the Greek word for Christ.

Christianity

SPREAD OF CHRISTIANITY IN WESTERN EUROPE

The Roman Empire went as far north as the Rhine and Danube rivers. Beyond them were heathen tribes. These tribes were always raiding the Empire. In AD 410 one of these tribes sacked Rome, and this was more or less the end of the great Roman Empire.

The Christian church in the West now had two tasks: to preserve as much as possible of Roman culture for the future, and to spread the Good News among these new tribes. These two tasks often went together.

We will look at the work of some great missionaries who preached Christ in what are now Britain, France, and Germany. It was from Ireland that the Gospel came to Scotland. St. Patrick had died in AD 494 after great success in preaching in Ireland. In AD 563 St. Columba set sail from Ireland in a small boat called a curragh. He landed on the island of Iona and built a monastery. There is still a monastery on Iona which belongs to the Iona Community, a band of modern Christians. From Iona St. Columba went over to mainland Scotland.

From Iona too St. Aidan went down into England where another island, Lindisfarne (Holy Island), became his centre. From Lindisfarne the Gospel spread through the north of England.

From Devon, further south in England, another great Christian, St. Boniface, took the Good News to Germany. At Geismar in Germany, Boniface began to cut down a tree sacred to the local god. Before he had finished a blast of wind blew down the rest of the tree and it broke into four pieces. The local people were impressed at this sign and later became Christians. Boniface built a small church in its place. He was killed by robbers while waiting to make some new Christians by a river. By AD 800 most of that part of Germany had become Christian.

Patrick, Columba, Aidan, and Boniface were all monks, and monks were very important in the western church. Monks had begun in Egypt where a rich young man, Anthony, heard a priest say in church the words from the Bible, 'Sell all you have, give to the poor, and follow me'. St. Anthony had done just that and gone out into the Egyptian desert to pray. After him came many other monks, and other orders of monks. They were reacting in part to the growing worldliness of the church. It seemed to them that the words of Jesus 'Be perfect, as your father in heaven is perfect' must be taken seriously. It was no good being half a Christian. The monks were wanting to lead a deeper spiritual life. They were copied by nuns who set up convents for women with the same aim.

Many orders came into being, that of St. Benedict (Benedictine Monks), was especially important. They believed in the power of prayers said together, they stressed meditation and silent prayer, they believed in the simple life, they did not marry, they did their work to the glory of God.

It was often monks and nuns who spread the Gospel in the new areas of Europe. Monks were often the scholars who passed on what was left of the culture of Rome together with the Good News about the Lord Jesus they loved. Spiritual persons often had a big influence upon very worldly people such as kings. When the king became Christian, often the whole tribe became Christian.

The Curragh was a boat made of wicker covered with skins. St. Columba and his monks travelled in such boats.

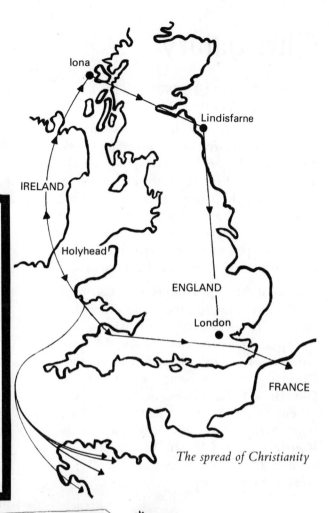

The spread of Christianity

St. Patrick's Prayer known as St. Patrick's
Breastplate
I arise today
through God's strength to pilot me
God's might to uphold me
God's wisdom to guide me
God's eye to look before me
God's ear to hear me
God's word to speak for me
God's hand to guide me
God's shield to protect me
God's host to secure me

The Cathedral on Iona

Christianity

SPREAD OF CHRISTIANITY IN EASTERN EUROPE

After the Western Empire with its centre in Rome was over-run by the invading tribes, the Roman Empire began to split into two. The Eastern Empire with its centre in Constantinople (named after Constantine) was not over-run. It defeated the invading tribes, and its form of Christianity spread and developed in a different way. Eastern Christianity also had great missionaries.

Two of the most famous were Cyril and Methodius. Through them and others like them the Gospel was taken into what is now Bulgaria, Hungary and Russia. In time, what we now call the Greek Orthodox Church came into being. The Orthodox Church whether Greek or Russian was different from the church that was growing in western Europe. We now call that the Roman Catholic Church. We will later look at the differences between the churches in west and east Europe.

SPREAD OF CHRISTIANITY IN ASIA AND AFRICA

The Good News was taken into the Delta area of Egypt where one of the main languages was Coptic. Christians in this area became known as Coptic Christians. They took the Good News further down into Africa. Some went to Ethiopia and began an Ethiopian Church that still exists today. Others went down the River Nile to what we now call the Sudan, and began the church there.

Nestorian Christians, who took their name from a Bishop of Constantinople named Nestorius, took the Gospel by land and by sea to Iran, India and China. Legend has it that St. Thomas, the disciple of Jesus (Doubting Thomas who wanted proof that Jesus had risen from the dead), went himself to India to tell people about Jesus. We know that there were Christians in India by the fourth century. They were there when modern missionaries came to India.

At the museum at Sian in China there is a famous stone tablet which tells the story of the coming of Christianity to China in AD 635. A Nestorian missionary 'a man of virtue named Alopen . . . after hardship and danger arrived at Sian . . . where the emperor received him as a guest in the palace'. The emperor gave the Christians a temple in Sian which was then the capital of China. By AD 781, when the stone tablet was written in the Chinese language, there were a good number of Christians in China.

By AD 1000 there were over a million Nestorian Christians, and over 200 Nestorian bishops, in places as far apart as Iran, Arabia, India, Central Asia, and China. Most of the Nestorian churches later died out. The countries in which they lived had been taken over by the Muslims. When the western Christians fought the Muslims at the time of the Crusades, the Nestorian Christians had a hard time. They became fewer and fewer. Asia's Christianity declined while Europe's grew.

The Church of St. Sophia, Kiev

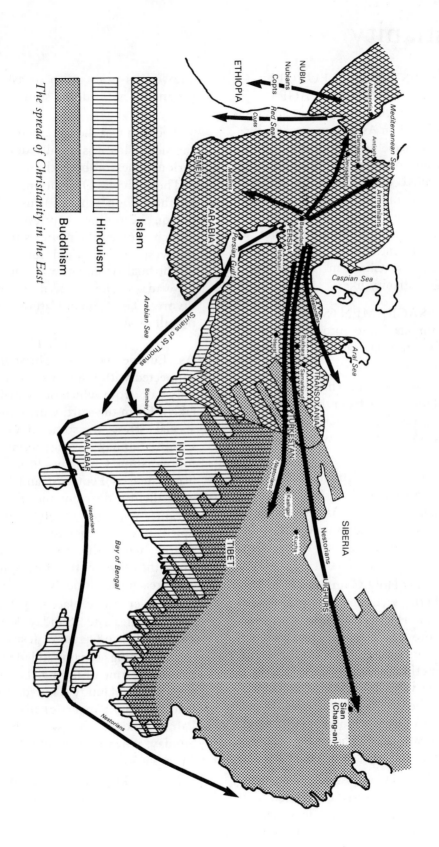

The spread of Christianity in the East

Islam

Hinduism

Buddhism

NUBIA
Nubians
Copts
ETHIOPIA
Copts
Red Sea
Mediterranean Sea
Alexandria
Antioch
Damascus
Jerusalem
Armenians
YEMEN
Medina
ARABIA
PERSIA
Baghdad
Isfahan
Persian Gulf
Caspian Sea
Arabian Sea
Syrians of St Thomas
Herat
Bukhara
Samarkand
TRANSOXANIA
Aral Sea
TURKESTAN
Nestorians
Bombay
MALABAR
INDIA
Kashgar
Kucha
SIBERIA
Nestorians
UIGHURS
Nestorians
TIBET
Bay of Bengal
Nestorians
Sian
(Chang-an)

13

Christianity

THE CHRISTIANS IN EUROPE DURING THE MIDDLE AGES

While the Coptic Church in Africa and the Nestorian Church in Asia grew weaker, the Churches in Europe became stronger. The Vikings from present-day Scandinavia, who had sailed their longboats around Europe to kill and burn wherever they went, now became Christians. The whole of Europe, West and East, became a Christian continent. Apart from Jews, everyone was a Christian. What was European Christianity like?

SACRAMENTS

Seven sacraments came into being. The churches of western and eastern Europe saw them a little differently.

The first was Baptism. This was mainly for babies. Holy water from the font in the church was used. The western church put more stress on baptism as washing away sin.

The second was Confirmation. The gift of the Holy Spirit was given to the person receiving this sacrament. After it, it was possible to take Holy Communion. It could be taken at a younger age in the eastern church.

The third was Holy Communion or the Eucharist. In this sacrament, the priest used bread and wine as Jesus had done at the Last Supper before his death. The western church, with its greater stress on the death of Christ, put this sacrament at the centre of its worship services. In the Mass, as it came to be called, the bread and wine were taken to become the body and blood of Christ and special bread was used. The eastern church emphasised it too but used ordinary bread.

The fourth was Confession or Penance. The eastern church stressed confession to a priest of one's faults and sins in order to remain right with God. The western church allowed its priests also to ask for acts of penance. That is doing something to show one is sorry.

The fifth was the sacrament of Anointing the sick. This was usually done in cases of serious illness in both churches.

The sixth was Ordination. This was done by the bishop who laid his hands on the person becoming a priest. The eastern church allowed their priests to be married, the western church did not.

The final sacrament was that of Marriage. Nowadays the eastern church allows divorce. The Roman Catholic church does not allow it.

FESTIVALS

As Europe became Christian, festivals connected with Jesus or the church became holy days from which our word holidays is taken. From the start, Christians had given special stress to some days and some seasons. Sunday was the special day set aside for worship. Christians took over Jewish feasts such as Pentecost and Passover but gave them a different meaning. Pentecost became Whitsun, the feast of the Holy Spirit. It looked back to the birthday of the church when the early Christians were given the power of the Holy Spirit to go out and preach the Good News about Jesus.

Passover was replaced by Easter. Good Friday and Easter Sunday looked to the death and rising again of Jesus.

Other things became added to Easter. For example a time of fasting (Lent) to prepare for Easter; Maundy Thursday when Jesus held the Last Supper for his disciples; and Palm Sunday, the week before Easter Sunday, when Jesus went into Jerusalem in triumph.

No one knew the exact day when Jesus was born. December 25th was made the church's birthday for Jesus in the West, and in the East, January 6th was chosen.

A font where baptism takes place

A priest leading the Eucharist

Festivals which celebrate the main events in the life of Jesus Christ.

Advent prepares for the coming of Christ (the Messiah). Christmas celebrates the birth of Jesus and is held on the 25th December in the West.

Lent is a period of spiritual discipline leading up to Easter.

Easter commemorates the death and resurrection of Jesus.

Ascension celebrates Jesus' ascension into heaven, held 40 days after Easter.

Pentecost marks the coming of the Holy Spirit, held 50 days after Easter.

A modern marriage ceremony

Christianity

EAST AND WEST CHURCHES FINALLY DISAGREE

There was a serious quarrel in AD 1054 when the leader of the western church, the Pope of Rome, had a fierce argument with the leader of the eastern church, the Patriarch of Constantinople. It was not until 1350 that the break between the two churches became final.

CHRISTIAN MINISTRY

The church had begun in a simple way when Jesus chose twelve disciples to be with Him. A hundred years after Jesus died the church had become more organised. Most Christians remained laymen, that is they did their everyday work but helped the church in their spare time. Some Christians spent their whole time serving the church. They were called ministers. Among them were three kinds of minister: the bishops who led the churches in areas that were called dioceses, the priests who led each church within a diocese, and deacons who helped the priest in the local church. Among the bishops, some were very important. In the West the bishop of Rome became most important of all and he became known as the Pope. In the East the bishops of four cities, above all Constantinople, became most important. They were known as Patriarchs. One reason for the divide between the churches was the Pope's claim to be head of the whole church. The East did not agree.

CHRISTIAN TEACHINGS

Great thinkers in East and West had summed up Christian beliefs. What did Christians believe about God? about Jesus Christ? about man? about the world? about the church? about the sacraments? about the future life? What was salvation? How could one get it? In creeds and books these thinkers, who were called theologians, gave answers to questions such as these. Two of these questions were very hard to solve: Who was God? and Who was Christ? Indeed these questions were linked.

Since the New Testament Christians had looked at Jesus and seen someone who was a man, yet someone who was also more than a man. These thinkers came to feel that Jesus was both man and God. But how could they put this into words that made sense? At the great Councils of the church such as Nicaea answers were given. The Christian beliefs were taught to the people.

In small ways East and West differed. The western church stressed the death of Jesus. That is why the crucifix became important. This was worn round the neck or hung on a wall. It showed the body of Jesus on the cross. It meant that Jesus had died for all persons and saved them from the sin that made them evil and kept them from God. The eastern church felt the risen Christ was more important than the dead Christ. On Easter Sunday they cry out 'Christ is risen! He is risen indeed!' If you go into a Greek Orthodox Church instead of crucifixes you will see icons. These are pictures of Jesus and the saints painted on wood. They do not show Christ suffering but in joy and triumph.

CHRISTIAN BUILDINGS

By this time great churches were built in all parts of Europe. Every town and village had its church, and the great towns had their cathedrals. Again East and West differed. Western churches had spires that pointed up into the sky. They pointed Christians away from this earth to God. Their grey walls said let us get away from this grey world of sin and struggle to the life of heaven. Eastern churches had domes rather than spires. Their domes and walls were often brightly coloured. This earth matters, they seemed to say. Jesus and the Holy Spirit have come down here to bring joy and light. They have come to change the earth.

Salisbury Cathedral with its magnificent spire

The Orthodox Church at Daphni, Greece

Roman Church monks wore the tonsure, their head shaved in the centre. Orthodox monks did not cut their hair.

An Orthodox Church icon

A Roman Church crucifix

St. Peter is often shown holding keys like these which represent the keys of heaven. He has been called the First Bishop of Rome and Roman Catholics believe that Jesus established the office of Pope when he said "And I say unto thee, that thou art Peter, and upon this rock will I build my Church."

Christianity

THE REFORMATION

In the sixteenth century there was a split in the western church into different churches with their own organisation, beliefs and view of the Bible. One cause of this division was a German called Martin Luther.

One day in 1505 he was almost struck by lightning. He was afraid because of this. He became a monk. But he was still afraid because he had no peace within. Another monk told him to read the Bible to find out about God. One day he read the words, 'The just shall live by faith'. He came to realise that by faith we can know God. He felt that the church was too rich and the Pope had too much power. He was very angry when a monk named Tetzel came to Germany to sell pardons for sin and to gain money for the church in Rome. Luther opposed these pardons, called indulgences. He wrote 95 famous theses or reasons against them, and nailed them on the door of Wittenburg church in Germany. The Pope was angry. Luther argued that God was known through Jesus Christ, and Jesus Christ was known through the Bible. So the Bible, not the Pope, was the key to faith. He translated the Bible from Latin into German so that many more people could read it. Through Luther's work the Lutheran Church became separate from the Roman Church.

Other reformers copied Luther. They looked for Jesus in the church and found it hard to find Him. They worked for the reform of the church. That is where the word Reformation comes from.

In 1536, a Frenchman, John Calvin, was asked to go to Geneva in Switzerland to teach and preach. He did not believe that churches should have bishops. A committee of ministers later called a Presbytery would be better.

In England and Scotland national churches came into being — the Church of England and the Church of Scotland. John Knox was a key figure in the Scottish Reformation. For two years he was a galley slave in a French ship. At another time he had to flee to Geneva where he met John Calvin. When he returned to Scotland he worked for a church based on Calvin's ideas. He wrote his plan for a Scottish Church in his works 'Confession of Faith' and 'Book of Discipline'. His ideas became the basis for the Church of Scotland. This church wanted nothing to do with the Pope, bishops, saints, set prayers, bright robes, ceremony, and the communion bread becoming the body of Christ.

In England the King became the head of the Church in England instead of the Pope but there were still archbishops and bishops, set prayers, robes, and ceremonies.

Robert Browne said that a reformed church should be separate from the state as well as from the Pope. Through his work the Congregational Church arose. He argued that true Christians should form their own churches. These should be separate from the state church. Each church, each congregation, should choose its own minister. The congregation itself would know the person God wanted to lead it.

In 1609 a group of people asked why babies who were too young to choose to be Christians should be baptised. Only adults who had put their faith in Christ could be baptised. People who believed in this were called Baptists.

The Reformers were also called Protestants. They protested against the faults of the Roman Church, but they protested and reformed in different ways. Reformation had come to the western church. So had division.

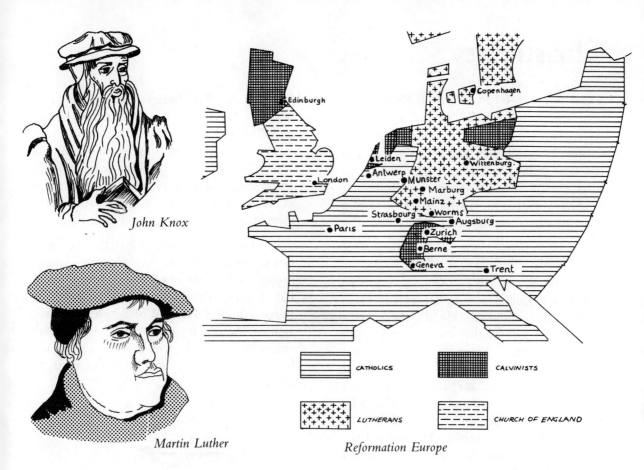

John Knox

Martin Luther

Reformation Europe

CATHOLICS

CALVINISTS

LUTHERANS

CHURCH OF ENGLAND

Two congregationalist preachers, Greenwood and Barrow, were executed at Tyburn in 1593 for sedition. They had spoken out against the King being the head of the Church.

Believer's Baptism
Only those who have shown that they have Christian faith can be baptised. The correct way to be baptised is by total immersion. In warm climates this can take place in the open air. In cold climates it takes place in a special baptistry.

Christianity

COUNTER-REFORMATION AND MISSIONS

At the Council of Trent, 1545-1563, the Roman Church became known as the Roman Catholic Church and began to reform itself. This was called the Counter-Reformation. Part of the Counter-Reformation was spreading the Good News to foreign lands. One of the leaders of this movement was Loyola.

Ignatius Loyola was born in Spain in 1491. He began life as a soldier. His aim was to become a general. He did become a general but not in the way he imagined. During a battle in Spain he broke his legs. Unable to walk, he read four books about Jesus and the saints that changed his life. For ten months, he lived in a cave. There he wrote much of his book on how to pray called 'Spiritual Exercises'. He formed the Society of Jesus and the rules of the Society were based on his book. He became General of the Society of Jesus in 1541 and it became known as the Jesuits. Part of the work of the Jesuits was to send missionaries to foreign lands.

A great Jesuit, Francis Xavier, was a pioneer missionary in Asia. He began work in India. He landed at Goa and worked among the Portugese who sailed there. Then he went to work among the poor Indians who spent their lives diving for pearls. Twenty thousand of them became Christians. He went to other parts of India, Ceylon, the East Indies, and finally Japan. As a result of his preaching about 150,000 people became Christians. By 1600 there were about half a million Christians in Japan. Then came a great persecution. Most of the Christians were tortured and killed, and the church almost died out.

In the other places where Xavier worked, the church did not die out. In India, Ceylon, Malaya, the East Indies, the church grew steadily. Xavier died in 1552 trying to get into China. Another Jesuit, Matthew Ricci, entered China in 1582. He studied Chinese and Confucian classics to try and understand the Chinese and speak to them in ways they could understand. Some important Chinese became Christians.

In Latin America Christianity was introduced by force. Some of the Jesuits brought Christian bravery and love as well. Las Casas, 1474-1566, worked for the Indians in the New World. He preached against the cruelty of some of the Spanish conquerors. He showed that friendship and love for the Indians would bring them to Christ.

Jesuit missionaries crucified at Nagasaki, Japan, in 1597

Francis Xavier was one of the early Jesuits. He landed in Goa, India, in 1542. Later he went to Japan and died trying to reach China.

Jesuits at the court of a Muslim ruler in India –

Teach us, good Lord, to serve thee as thou deservest
to give and not to count the cost
to fight and not to heed the wounds
to toil and not to ask for rest
to labour and not to ask for any reward save
knowing that we do thy will
Through Jesus Christ our Lord.

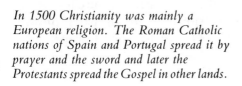

In 1500 Christianity was mainly a European religion. The Roman Catholic nations of Spain and Portugal spread it by prayer and the sword and later the Protestants spread the Gospel in other lands.

Christianity

PROTESTANT CHURCHES AND MISSIONS

In North America, Protestant Christians became very strong. Groups of people in Britain wanted freedom to worship as they pleased. They sailed to the newly discovered lands of North America.

THE PILGRIM FATHERS

The Pilgrim Fathers were looking for this freedom of worship. In 1620 they left Britain and went to North America. They sailed on a ship called the Mayflower. Before they landed in New England, they signed the Mayflower Pact. They promised to set up a new colony with just and equal laws. Free worship went along with equal laws. Christianity went hand in hand with what was later called democracy.

They called their first real settlement after Plymouth in Devon. At first their life was hard. For a year it was doubtful whether they would survive. They had help from the American Indians and by the end of the year it was clear that this small band of Christians would live and prosper. They held a special service of Thanksgiving. They thanked God for giving them enough to eat. They thanked God for helping them to survive. To this day the people of the United States keep the festival of Thanksgiving.

THE QUAKERS

The American state of Pennsylvania is named after William Penn. He was a Quaker. The Quakers, also called the Society of Friends, were another group who went to America to seek freedom of worship. They were honest in all things. They believed in peace.

In the Society of Friends there are no ministers, sacraments, or formal worship. They believe that all people should follow their own 'inner light'. At the worship in their meeting houses, there is no set order of worship. If people are moved by their 'inner light' they speak or sing or pray. If not, it does not matter. There can be complete silence.

THE METHODISTS

Methodism arose out of the work of John and Charles Wesley. As students at Oxford, they had formed a group to study and practise Christianity. There was method in their use of time and their study of the Bible. Other students mocked them and called them Methodists. The name 'Methodist' stuck. When the Wesleys left Oxford, they went to Georgia as missionaries. They had little success. They returned to England disappointed. One night John Wesley went to a small meeting at Aldersgate Street in London. He felt his heart strangely warmed. He found a new trust in Christ. For the rest of his life he rode around Britain preaching the Gospel.

His brother Charles wrote great hymns. They stressed that the Gospel was for all people. 'For all, for all, my Saviour died. For all my Lord was crucified', they said. The aim of life was to love God and our fellows. They used ordinary folk who were laymen to lead their societies and to preach. The Methodist Church grew in Britain. In America it grew like wildfire. The American Methodist Church was set up at Baltimore in 1784.

As Americans moved out West, Methodist preachers moved with them to the frontiers. In 70 years 1½ million Americans became Methodists. The Methodists became one of the largest Protestant Churches in America.

The Methodist message, 'the Good News is for all', inspired Protestant missions. Soon all the Protestant Churches were sending missionaries to all parts of the world. The Gospel had left Europe. The Christian religion had become a world religion.

The Mayflower

The Pilgrim Fathers

When George Fox, the founder of the Society of Friends, was being tried for holding religious meetings he warned the judge to "Tremble at the Word of the Lord". The judge mocked Fox and his followers by calling them Quakers (tremblers).

John Wesley preaching at the market cross

William Penn founded the colony of Pennsylvania as a home for Quakers in 1681.

Christianity

CHRISTIAN ETHICS AND SOCIAL REFORM

From the start, Christians stressed good living. Jesus said, 'Always treat others as you would like them to treat you' (Matthew 7:12); 'Love your enemies' (Matthew 5:9). He said when people are hungry, feed them; when they are naked, give them clothes; when they are in need, help them. In his parables, he gave examples. He told the story of a man going from Jerusalem to Jericho who was beaten up by robbers. People who should have known better were too busy or too afraid to help. In the end it was a Samaritan who gave his time, his money and his love to help the man. If you want to follow me, go and do the same, said Jesus. Be like the Good Samaritan. Care for others.

When missionaries went to other lands, they not only preached and taught. They set up hospitals to heal the sick. They set up schools to educate. They tried to help the poor and needy. In India, they helped the Indians to get rid of suti, the burning of widows while still alive with the bodies of their dead husbands. In our own day, Mother Theresa works among the poor of Calcutta in India. She brings up orphans when there is nobody else to look after them. In this way she shows that the Gospel is to do with the body as well as the soul. It is doing good as well as believing. It is loving persons as well as God. It shows that Jesus has an interest in the whole of life.

Another example is the struggle to end slavery. The Quakers and Methodists had spoken against the slave trade. It was another Christian, William Wilberforce, who worked to end it.

He met a man called John Newton who had been the captain of a slave ship. This ship carried slaves from Africa to the sugar and tobacco plantations in America. Some of the slaves died on the ship due to the awful conditions. If they lived, when they reached America they were sold as slaves. They belonged to someone else. They had to work for them. They had no human rights.

During a great storm, Newton said that if he survived the storm he would follow Christ. He lived, became a minister, and spoke about the evils of the slave trade to Wilberforce. Wilberforce was horrified by the story of the slaves and vowed to spend his life putting an end to the slave trade. Through his work, slavery was abolished in 1807.

In our own day, an American Black Christian, Dr. Martin Luther King, worked to bring equal rights to black people (the former slaves) in America. In the end he was shot. But he had won equal rights for his people.

In Britain, other Christians set up schools for poor children (like John Pound's 'Ragged Schools'), or orphanages for children without parents (like Dr. Barnardo's Homes). Another kind of church was set up to help the poor. It was called the Salvation Army and was led by William Booth.

He wrote a book 'In Darkest England and the Way Out'. He pointed out that the poor in Britain needed helping as well as the slaves in Africa. The poor were not welcomed in wealthy churches. They had little money and poor houses. In a pub it was warm and bright and they went there and got drunk. The Salvation Army, in the name of Jesus, declared war on this poverty and misery.

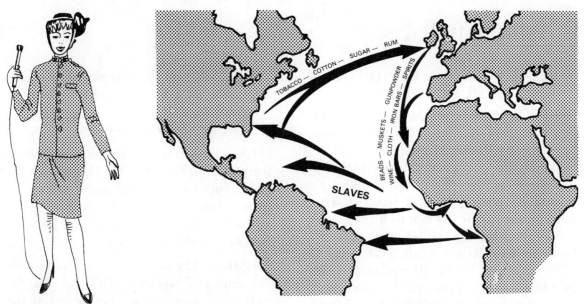

The Salvationists preached Christ and gave hope. They sang bright hymns and songs. They wore bright uniforms. They played drums. They spoke in words that the people could understand. They also set up children's homes. They helped drunkards and prisoners. They set up maternity homes, farms, and hospitals. They not only preached the words of the Good News, they also did the deeds of the Gospel. This has been true of Christian ethics and social reform since the beginning of the church.

The slave triangle. Goods were sent from Europe to Africa to obtain slaves. Slaves were taken to America and sold. With the money for the slaves more goods were bought to bring back to Europe.

The Drunkard's Children in the Gin Shop, from a drawing by the artist Cruikshank. It was to this kind of place that poor people went to drink to escape the miseries of their everyday life.

The badge of the Salvation Army

Christianity

RELIGION, SCIENCE AND THE SECULAR WORLD

Charles Darwin. Charles Darwin planned to be a minister of the church. He went on a sea voyage in the Pacific. His job was to gather and study the plants and animals he found out there. He never became a minister. Instead he became a great scientist. His work in the Pacific led him to form a new theory about the world. He saw that plants, birds, and animals were slightly different on different islands and in different places. He asked why. He answered because they changed to suit the different conditions. They adapted to where they were. They evolved. He wrote about his work, and his new theory of evolution, in 1859 in 'The Origin of Species'. He argued that life had changed and evolved over millions of years from simple plant life, to animals, to man.

The problem was that the Bible did not seem to agree. It said that all things were made as they are now. They had not evolved.

Christians came to see the truth of Darwin's work. They saw that the Bible was not a book of science. It was a book of spiritual truth.

Sigmund Freud. Freud raised questions about man himself. Christians had said that man had a soul. This was the part of man that was most important. They had said that man was sinful. He was sinful because Adam, the first man, had sinned. Adam's original sin was part of all men.

Freud put things in a different way. His science was what we call psychology. He, as it were, looked inside the soul of man. As well as the self we know about, he said, there is another self we do not know about. It is our unconscious self. It is hidden inside us. If we want to know about it, we can.

Freud also said that our parents are very important in our lives. What happened to us when we were children was vital. It tells us why we are the people we are.

Christians came to see there was some truth in Freud's work. He taught us a lot about ourselves. What happens to us does matter, especially what happened to us when we were children. Freud gave us insight into the soul and sin.

Karl Marx. The work of Marx was another challenge to Christians. Marx looked at the ugly cities around him. He looked at the long hours of work and the poor people who did most of the work. He felt this was unfair and unjust. He found a new theory to explain the poverty of the working class. He said that the order of society was wrong. Its structure was unfair. Society must change. The working class must have more power. The rich people, the capitalists, must have less.

Some Christians came to see some truth in Marx's work. They saw that it was not the will of God that poor people should suffer or starve. Some of the divisions in society were wrong. The problem was that Marxism (Communism) denied God altogether. Christians said this was wrong. It would lead to a lack of freedom and human rights.

The church then accepted the truths in the work of Darwin, Freud and Marx. Christians saw the Bible, man, and society in a new way. The greatness of God, the nature of man, and the love of Christ were better understood.

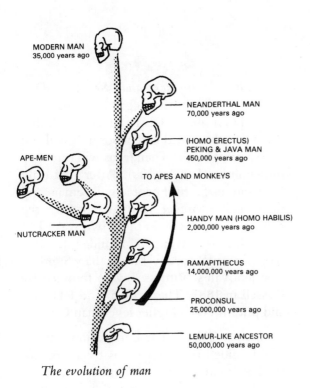

MODERN MAN
35,000 years ago

NEANDERTHAL MAN
70,000 years ago

(HOMO ERECTUS)
PEKING & JAVA MAN
450,000 years ago

APE-MEN

TO APES AND MONKEYS

HANDY MAN (HOMO HABILIS)
2,000,000 years ago

NUTCRACKER MAN

RAMAPITHECUS
14,000,000 years ago

PROCONSUL
25,000,000 years ago

LEMUR-LIKE ANCESTOR
50,000,000 years ago

The evolution of man

Charles Darwin was at first opposed for his theory of evolution. Here he is pictured as an ape himself.

Karl Marx

Sigmund Freud

Christianity

NEW CHRISTIAN GROUPS OUTSIDE THE MAIN CHURCHES

In the last hundred years new Christian groups have arisen. Some of them are outside the main churches. As we will see, the main churches have come closer together.

The differences between the Roman Catholic, Protestant and Orthodox Churches have got less. The new cults are often very different.

Christian Scientists. They were founded by Mary Baker Eddy in 1866. She had been ill. When reading the Bible she felt much better. It seemed to her that in the Bible were laws for good health. She wrote about these laws in 'Science and Health with Key to the Scriptures'. She said that God was good, and his creation was good. Suffering and illness were not made by God. Health and goodness were real. Sickness was not. Through faith and understanding sickness would go. The Christian Scientists have more faith in their own experts than in doctors. The centre of their work is in Boston, USA.

Mormons. They were founded by Joseph Smith in 1830. They are also known as the Latter Day Saints. Smith claimed to find some golden plates upon which were written the Book of Mormon. With the Bible, this became the holy book of the Mormons. After Smith's death in 1844, Brigham Young led the Mormons on an epic journey across America. When they came to Salt Lake City he cried 'This is the place!' It became and remains their centre. They give two years of their lives to missionary service. They give a tenth of their money to the church. They do not smoke or drink. They say that at the end of time, most people will find salvation.

Jehovah's Witnesses and Seventh Day Adventists. Both these groups stress the Second Coming of Christ. They think that the end of the world will be soon. It will end with a great battle. Then Jesus will rule for a millennium (1,000 years). After that only God and his faithful people will remain and they will live forever. Both groups stress the Bible but interpret it in their own way. The Seventh Day Adventists, founded in 1863, worship on Saturday rather than Sunday. The Jehovah's Witnesses were founded by Russell in 1881. They called God Jehovah, and put him on a higher level than Christ.

Unification Church. The Unification Church was founded in recent times by a Korean, the Reverend Moon. Its members are called the Moonies. They oppose communism which they say is godless. They say Mr. Moon is a prophet through whom God speaks.

These cults oppose the main churches, and think that ordinary Christians are weak. Christians of the main churches have something to learn from them. For they know what they believe. They know their scriptures, they know the Bible. They are keen and enthusiastic. They want to witness to their faith. They are good at using magazines and books to tell others about their beliefs. They have strong sense of urgency. They give a big place to ordinary laymen. They train their members in how to speak to other people about their beliefs. They are not afraid of being laughed at. If the early Christians were alive now, they would disagree with the ideas of the cults but agree with their zeal.

Each Sunday the same message is heard in Christian Science churches across the world. It is sent from Boston, USA and read everywhere including this church near London.

Mary Baker Eddy

Jehovah's Witnesses go from door to door spreading their beliefs.

The Mormon Temple at Salt Lake City

Christianity

THE CHURCHES BEGIN TO UNITE

During this century the main groups of Christians have come closer together. The call for unity began on the mission field. The splits in the church had come in Europe. But these splits between churches that seemed important in Europe did not matter very much to Africans or Asians. Jesus was important to Indian or Japanese Christians. Separate churches, whether they were Roman Catholic, Orthodox, Church of England, Church of Scotland, Lutheran, Presbyterian, Congregationalist, Baptist, Quaker, Salvation Army, Methodist, were less important. They were confusing. If Christians loved each other, why were they separate? If Jesus was the One Lord of the Church, why were the churches separate?

In 1948 at Amsterdam in Holland the World Council of Churches was formed. All the Protestant Churches met together in one body. Following this, united churches were set up in different lands. The Church of South India brought together Methodists, Presbyterians, Congregationalists, and Anglicans (Church of England) in South India. Other united churches were formed in North India, Canada, Australia, and many other places.

Although not in the World Council of Churches, the Roman Catholic Church has in recent years come much closer to the Orthodox Church and the Protestant Churches. The Pope has met the Patriarch of the Orthodox Church, the Archbishop of Canterbury, the Moderator of the Church of Scotland and leaders of other Churches.

There are Christians in every land of the world with the possible exceptions of Tibet and Afghanistan. The church is no longer European. It is a World Church. In the Gospels Jesus said, 'Go and teach all nations, baptising them in the name of the Father, and of the Son, and of the Holy Spirit' (Matthew 28:19); 'I pray . . . that they all may be one . . . that the world may believe' (John's Gospel 17:21).

As the church becomes a world church, it becomes a more united church. In all the churches, an important leaflet is being discussed. It is called, 'Baptism, Eucharist and Ministry'. Should there be baptism for children or adults? Do the bread and the wine of the eucharist *remind* us of Christ's body and blood shed on the cross, or do they *become* the body and blood of Christ in the service? Should there be bishops?

These are some of the issues that caused the churches to split. Leading thinkers in those churches have written a leaflet *together* in the hope that the churches will unite more closely than ever before. They know they have one Lord, one faith, one baptism.

Pope John XXIII called the Second Vatican Council to reform the Roman Catholic Church.

The badge of the Ecumenical Movement

John 17, v 20-21
"But it is not for these alone that I pray, but for those also who through their words put their faith in me; may they all be one."

METHODIST

ANGLICAN

ROMAN CATHOLIC

ORTHODOX

LUTHERAN

UNITED REFORMED CHURCH CONGREGATIONAL AND PRESBYTERIAN

BAPTIST

PRESBYTERIAN

SALVATION ARMY

SOCIETY OF FRIENDS

Christians are divided into many Churches. Here are ten of the Churches, drawn in a network. A net is a symbol of unity. Will these Churches ever be one Church?

Christianity

CHRISTIANITY AND WORLD AFFAIRS

When men first stood on the moon, they looked back at ONE earth. From space, it looked like a global village. In a village, the lives of the villagers are linked. It is the same in the world as a whole. No person, no nation, is an island separate from the others. We are all in it together.

Christians have a deep interest in world affairs because God is the God of the whole world. Jesus died for all men. God created the earth and has a concern for it. Man can destroy himself. He can also work with others to build a better world.

Two problems stand out, Nuclear War and Saving the Earth. In 1945 the first atomic bombs were dropped on Hiroshima and Nagasaki in Japan. They were very small but they destroyed those cities. Since then nuclear weapons have become more deadly. There are more than 50,000 of them. If most of them were used in a nuclear war they would destroy much of the earth itself. Christians are giving new thought to the question of peace. The Pope, the World Council of Churches, and church leaders in different lands are speaking about it. They do not always agree on the answer. They agree that the nuclear threat is serious.

Christians are thinking more about the earth. In the past, Christians have thought more about God and man than about the earth. Now they are thinking about the earth. How can the earth be saved? How can we care for the earth rather than abuse it? These questions are now important.

In recent years Christians have talked much more with people of other religions. When Christian missionaries went to Asia, they met people of other religions. They met Hindus in India, Muslims in the Middle East, Buddhists in South East Asia. They met Sikhs, Taoists, Confucians and Shintoists. They converted some. They found that others had faith, and that they knew God. They found that other religions had created great cultures, just as Christianity had.

All religions are important. To build a world of peace and harmony needs the help of all religions. People of all religions meeting and talking together is very important. We hope this book will help.

In a nuclear war the earth and its people are at stake

NO CRUISE

CHRISTIAN CND

NB

WE WANT BREAD NOT CAKE

The rich North needs to be persuaded to help the poor South

An African National Park where animals are still safe

Buddhist Dalai Lama meeting young people in the West

Judaism

Judaism is the religion of the Jews. A person is a Jew if his or her mother is a Jew. In their early days, the Jews lived in Palestine where they had a kingdom called Judah. In Roman times this was known as Judea, so that the people from Judea were the Jews and their religious beliefs Judaism.

The Jews believe that God made a bargain or covenant with their ancestor Abraham. Even today, if a non-Jew is converted to Judaism, he or she has to go through a ceremony of being adopted into the Jewish family as a child of Abraham.

MOSES AND JEWISH FESTIVALS

Moses was the most important person in the early history of the Jews. The three main festivals of the Jews record the great deeds of Moses. These also fit in with the dates of the three harvests in the old days of Palestine: Passover was the time of the barley harvest, Pentecost the time of the wheat harvest, and Tabernacles the time of the grape and olive harvest.

Passover is in memory of the early Jews being freed from slavery in Egypt. Jews remember how Moses, as a baby, was saved and brought up by an Egyptian princess. As a young man he killed an Egyptian slave-master and fled across the Red Sea to the land of Midian. Here he heard God telling him to lead the Jews out of Egypt into a land flowing with milk and honey, the land that had been promised to Abraham and his family.

Moses went back to Egypt and asked the Pharoah to let him take the Jews away but the Pharoah of Egypt would not let the Jews leave. Moses told Pharoah that the angel of death would visit Egypt and the first-born human or animal would die. Moses told the Jews to kill a first-born lamb and smear the doorposts of their houses with its blood so that the angel of death would 'pass-over' Jewish houses and not kill anyone. After this Pharoah told Moses to take the people away. This is known as the Exodus, when Moses led the Jews out of Egypt. The Passover recalls these events. At this festival the Jews eat roast lamb with bitter herbs to remind them of their suffering and they also eat unleavened bread.

Pentecost, 'Shavuoth', takes place seven weeks after Passover when the synagogue is decorated with fruit and flowers as in a harvest festival. It recalls how Moses led the Jews to the foot of Mount Sinai in the land of Midian. He climbed the mountain to be with God. He came down bringing with him the Ten Commandments. This is the beginning of the Law or Torah which is the most important part of the Jewish religion.

Tabernacles, 'Sukkoth', is a reminder of the time when the Jews lived in small shelters or tabernacles. For forty years they wandered in the country between Egypt and Canaan. They needed shelters in the wilderness. Modern Jews recall this as they put models of shelters or tabernacles in their homes and decorate them with fruit, flowers and branches.

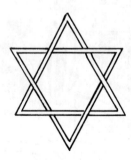

The six pointed star, the symbol of Judaism

34

Inside a Synagogue.
An orthodox synagogue, British type. The holy ark is on the east side towards Jerusalem. In front of it and above the pulpit is the lamp of perpetual light. In the middle of the synagogue is a raised stand known as the Bimah. From it the Minister or the Cantor or whoever is leading the prayers conducts the service.

The Torah is carried in procession from the Ark to the Bimah for the reading of the holy word.

In Orthodox synagogues the men sit downstairs and the women and children in the gallery.

Repairing the Torah. Torah are never thrown away. If they cannot be repaired they are carefully preserved, for they contain the word and name of God.

Judaism

LATER HISTORY

The Jews entered the Promised Land of Palestine under Joshua. Under kings, such as David and Solomon, they grew in strength and they built the temple in Jerusalem. Their prophets, such as Isaiah and Jeremiah, made them see that their God was God of the whole world, not just the God of the Jews. There were two sides to God's relationships with the Jews. On the one side, the Jews were God's chosen people. On the other side, the Jews were called to follow God and obey him.

In 586 BC Nebuchadnezzar, the king of Babylon, destroyed Jerusalem and the temple. He took away the Jews to exile in Babylon. Later kings allowed the Jews to return and they rebuilt the temple. The country became part of the Roman Empire. In AD 70 when the Jews rebelled against the Romans, the Romans destroyed Jerusalem and sent most of the Jews away from Palestine. In the Second World War in what is called the Nazi Holocaust 6 million out of 12 million Jews died. In AD 1948, the state of Israel was set up in Palestine. The Jews once again had a country of their own.

HOLY BOOKS AND THE TORAH

The holy book of the Jews is the Jewish Bible which is the same as the Christian Old Testament. The most important part of it is the first five books, Genesis, Exodus, Leviticus, Numbers and Deuteronomy. These are called the Pentateuch. They are supposed to have been written by Moses and are the beginning of the Torah, which means the Law or the Teachings. They tell the story of how God gave this Law to Moses on Mount Sinai.

In addition to the Ten Commandments, there were many other teachings and laws — laws of marriage, crime and punishment, what to eat and what not to eat, religious practices, holy days and other matters so that the Jews could live together in peace.

In addition to the written Law, there also grew up an oral or spoken Law. These spoken laws had to be adapted to fit the needs of the Jews living in different countries. The adaptations were made by the Rabbis. They became the leaders of groups of Jewish people in different parts of the world. In the 6th century AD the spoken laws were written down in another holy book called the Talmud. Over the years there have been many laws and interpretations of laws, and the Talmud is now in many volumes.

Studying the Torah and living by the Torah is the most important thing in Judaism.

The Torah

A page from a Spanish Haggadah written in the 14th century. It shows part of the Passover service with the Israelites as slaves in Egypt.

Matzoth–pieces of unleavened bread for the passover, hung on a rail before being put into the oven

Dietary law set out in the Torah. All meat must be Kosher, that is, drained of blood. The laws were necessary to keep the Israelites healthy during the many years they spent in the hot desert before reaching the promised land.

What to eat and what not to eat.

Leviticus 11 verse 2

These are the beasts which ye shall eat

Leviticus 11 verse 4

Nevertheless these shall ye not eat

Judaism

JEWISH WORSHIP

The Jewish place of worship is called a synagogue. There must be at least ten male Jews present for a proper service. In an orthodox synagogue, the men and women are separated, the men going into the main assembly hall on the ground floor, the women watching the service from the women's gallery.

The Sabbath day, from sunset Friday evening to sunset Saturday evening, is a reminder of the creation of the world. In the home, candles are lit at sunset and the men go to the synagogue. They return home for the evening meal, the best of the week. Next morning the family go to the synagogue. At morning prayer and at festivals the worshippers wear a Tallith. This is a white silken or woollen cloth with fringes, with blue or black stripes at the ends. Some worshippers put on Tefillin (Phylacteries). These are two small leather boxes containing passages from the holy books fastened to the wrist by a leather strap.

The chief prayer at the service is the Shema: 'Hear, O Israel, the Lord our God, The Lord is One.' It sums up much of Jewish faith. Then comes the Amidah which consists of eighteen blessings.

The reading of the Torah is the important part of the service and the whole of the Torah is read through every year. There may also be readings from the Prophets or from the Psalms. The head of the Jewish people in the district, the Rabbi, gives a talk or sermon. The sermon helps people to think about their religion, what it means and how it can help them in their daily life.

Two important days which few Jews will miss are 'Rosh Hashanah', the New Year, and 'Yom Kippur'. New Year is reckoned as the time to look back over the old year and to start with a clean sheet. On this day the Shofar, a ram's horn, is blown.

The main holy day is Yom Kippur, the Day of Atonement. It is a sabbath of fasting and rest. Four times during the day a list of sins is recited. The story of the scapegoat is told. This is the kid of a goat on which the nation's sins were placed. It was then chased away. The nation's sin had gone and the people could start with a clean sheet. After the story there are prayers for the forgiveness of sins. Elijah's saying about God being the one true God is read. A blast on the Shofar ends the day.

RITUALS

Four rituals are important for Jews.

The first is circumcision. At the age of eight days, Jewish boys are circumcised. This is a mark of being a Jew.

The second is Bar-Mitzvah. This is a special service and a time of great joy in Jewish families. From then on a Jewish boy can take part in worship and count as a full member of the Jewish community.

The third ritual is that of marriage. Because to Jews the family is important, the marriage ceremony is very significant.

The last ritual is that of burial. For seven days after a burial, known as shivah, the mourners of the dead person stay at home. Family members, even if they live far away, try to 'go to the shivah'. The family is central to all these rituals. It is through the strength of the family that Jews have survived and grown.

The synagogue in the university at Jerusalem.

Tallith (Shawl)

Tefillin (Phylacteries)

A synagogue in London

Bar-Mitzvah means in Hebrew "a son of the commandment". It is also the ceremony of religious confirmation. The boy will have learned to translate parts of the Pentateuch and prophetic readings which he will recite in the synagogue on the sabbath nearest to his 13th birthday. He is then considered an adult member of the Jewish community.

39

Judaism

SCHOOLS OF THOUGHT IN JUDAISM

Orthodox Jews are faithful to the ancient traditions. They believe that the Torah was written by Moses, inspired by God. They live by the laws of the Jewish Bible and the Talmud. They obey the instructions of the Torah about what they should or should not eat, and they do not work on the Sabbath. They use the Hebrew language in the synagogue services, and they run schools for their children where they teach them Hebrew. They believe that the old ways are mainly right.

Reform Jews are more liberal. Like modern Christian scholars, they interpret the Torah in the light of modern research. The services in the synagogue often have organ music and a choir. Families sit together, and while part of the service is in Hebrew the sermon is in English.

Conservative Jews are a mid-way movement between Orthodox and Reform Jews and they are strong in the United States. They respect the Torah but interpret it in the light of modern knowledge. They continue the traditional forms and the use of Hebrew in the synagogue. They do necessary work on the Sabbath Day, but also make it a time of thought and prayer.

The *Hasidic Jews* started in Poland about 200 years ago. They believe in a direct approach to God through personal experience and prayer. A famous spiritual book called the Kabbalah had stressed a more inward religion in the thirteenth century. Modern Hasidism feels the same need to know and practise the presence of God.

Zionism was founded in 1896 by Theodor Herzl. He wanted the Jews to return to Palestine and set up their own state. The Zionists and other groups worked hard for many years. In 1948 the state of Israel was set up. After 2,500 years the Jews had their own home again.

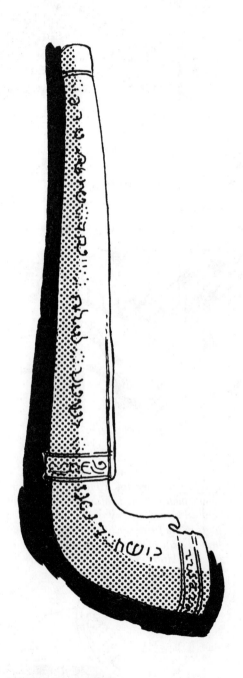

Ram's horn or Shofar which is blown at the New Year Service

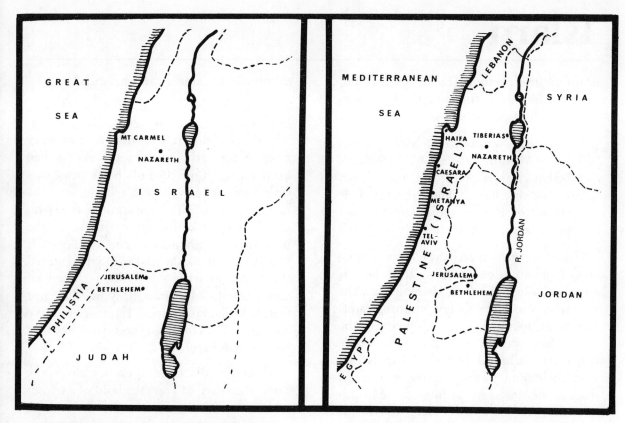

The Kingdom of Israel and Judah about 850 B.C.

Palestine and Jordan after Partition, 1948

Menorah – a candle holder with seven branches to give continual light. It is a symbol of Judaism.

Islam

Islam means 'to submit' to the will of God. People who follow this faith are known as Muslims, 'those who submit'.

Muhammad was born in Mecca in AD 570. When Muslims mention Muhammad's name they immediately add the words 'Peace be on him'. This shows their veneration for him as the greatest of the prophets and the founder of their religion.

His father was a merchant who was often away from home on business. While he was away at Yathrib, he died. He never saw the son who was born a few months later. Mecca, at this time, was a holy city to the Arabs. In it was the well, Zamzam, where Hagar and Ishmael refreshed themselves after their long journey across the desert from Palestine. According to Muslim tradition, Abraham came there to visit his son, Ishmael, and together they built the Kaaba — the place of God. In the wall of the Kaaba, Abraham put a small oval stone, about seven inches long. This stone is said to have come from Paradise and to have been snow white. Now it is jet black after having been kissed by millions of pilgrims since it was first set up over 3,000 years ago.

At the time of Muhammad's birth the Arabs had become idol worshippers and in the Kaaba many idols were to be found. Arabs came from all over Arabia to worship the idols, and from these pilgrims the people of Mecca made a lot of money. In his early childhood, Muhammad was sent to live in the desert with a family of wandering Bedouin shepherd folk. Many town Arabs would send their children to these Bedouin for a few months or years. Muhammad stayed with them until he was six. He went back to his mother. After a few months she died. Muhammad went with his uncle, who was a merchant, and on his journeys he probably met both Jews and Christians. He eventually became a caravan leader.

Muhammad was well liked, an honest, fair-minded man who could be trusted. There is a tradition that while he was away from Mecca, the wall of the Kaaba had been damaged and the holy black stone was dislodged. The wall was rebuilt, and the chief men of the city were arguing as to who should have the honour of replacing the holy stone. They nearly came to blows. It was agreed to ask the first man who entered the Kaaba to settle the problem. They sat and waited. Muhammad, who had just finished a caravan trip, came in to give thanks to Allah for his safe return. They told him the problem.

'Place the Black stone on my cloak,' he said, 'then each of you take hold of a corner and you will all share in the honour of carrying the stone to its place.' This they did. As they reached the wall Muhammad quickly put the stone in position before anyone could start another argument. Everyone began to praise the wise man who had solved a difficult problem.

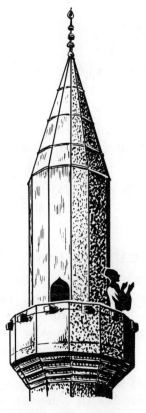

A Muslim place of worship is called a Mosque. Domes and minarets (pencil like towers) are features of mosques.

A Muslim is called to prayer five times a day from the minaret. The man who does the calling is known as a Muezzin.

Islam has spread from West Africa to Indonesia and China; from parts of the USSR to Tanzania.

Islam

Not long afterwards, Muhammad married Khadijah, a wealthy widow of forty, fifteen years older than himself. The marriage was very happy. Until Khadijah died, Muhammad did not marry again, although to have several wives was an Arab custom.

At that time Muhammad began to think more and more about religion and less and less about his business as a caravan leader and merchant. He often spent many days in a cave in the desert coming home for a while and then returning to the loneliness of the cave. While there he had a vision. The angel Gabriel appeared to him and said, 'O Muhammad, truly thou art the messenger of Allah and I am his angel Gabriel'. After this, the angel Gabriel appeared to him many times and told him the laws which were later written down in the Koran.

Muhammad returned to Mecca and began to preach 'There is but one God, Allah'. (The word, Allah, is a shortened form of al-ilah, the God.) The people of the city were angry; they could see that if Muhammad had his way, all idols would be destroyed and with them would go the money they made. They tried to kill Muhammad. He fled to friends in Yathrib. The flight to Yathrib in AD 622 is taken as the starting point for the Muslim calendar. The flight is known as Hijra, sometimes spelt as Hegira, and all Muslim dates are AH — Anno Hegira — 'after the flight'. The Muslim year is a lunar year of 354 days.

Yathrib became known as 'the City of the Prophet' — shortened to Medina (City). The people of Mecca came to kill him, but the people of Medina supported Muhammad and defeated them. Muhammad stayed in Medina eight years, training the people to be missionaries. He then returned to and conquered Mecca. He destroyed all the idols in the Kaaba and declared Mecca to be the holy place of God.

He continued his work of conversion among the Meccan Arabs, and trained many of them to go as missionaries among the other Arabs.

Two years after he entered Mecca, Islam had spread throughout Arabia. In AD 632, or AH 10, Muhammad died.

THE SPREAD OF ISLAM

After the Prophet had died, his followers met to elect a successor — a Caliph. They needed someone who could enforce the law, lead in war and guide in peace. Abu Bakr, one of Muhammad's closest friends, and one of the first of the believers, became the first Caliph. He did not live long. Before he died he named another of Muhammad's friends, Umar, as the second Caliph.

Umar has been called the second founder of Islam, for while he was Caliph the Muslim armies captured Damascus (AD 635), Jerusalem (AD 636), Egypt (AD 640), and had spread Islam through Persia to the borders of India by the year AD 644.

In the next century the all-conquering Muslim armies spread along the north coast of Africa and over-ran Spain. They crossed the Pyrenees and were only prevented from conquering France by Charles Martel, who defeated them at the Battle of Tours in AD 732. The Muslims remained in Spain until the fifteenth century. From the Muslim universities in North Africa and Spain, new ideas came on astronomy, chemistry, medicine, anatomy, mapmaking, and navigation.

The Muslims spread eastwards from Persia to India. Here, from AD 1000, they had carved for themselves a great empire, with the capital at Delhi. From there they

The holy cities of the Muslims

Mecca	*Birthplace of Muhammad 570 A.D. Muslims pray towards Mecca*
Medina	*The place to which Muhammad fled for safety*
Jerusalem	*Muhammad prayed there in his famous night journey*

The Arabs trace their descent from Abraham through his marriage to Hagar and their son Ishmael. Hagar and Ishmael were turned out of Abraham's camp because Sarah, Abraham's other wife was jealous of Hagar.

Hagar = Abraham = Sarah

Ishmael   Isaac

The twelve tribes of the Desert (The Arabs)   *The twelve tribes of Israel (The Jews)*

The Holy Sword–A strange two pronged sword known as "the Cleaver" was worn by Muhammad in battle. It is shown here on a 15th century Turkish banner.

A rosary and a mosque lamp

Lamps like this were used in mosques before electricity. Words from the Koran are used in the decoration. There are ninety-nine names for God in the Koran so Muslims use a rosary of ninety-nine beads to help them remember them in their prayers.

Islam

spread, not by conquest but by trade, eastwards to Malaysia, Indonesia and China. Arab traders carried the message of Islam across the jungles and grasslands of Central Africa to the West Coast. Today, the religion stretches across the whole of Africa and Asia in a broad belt.

The problem of who should be Caliph has broken Islam into two big groups or sects — the Sunnis, the orthodox or traditional Muslims who follow the elected Caliph; and the Shiites, who believe that the Caliph should have been chosen from amongst the members of Muhammad's family and that his son-in-law, Ali, should have stayed Caliph. They believe that the descendants of Ali are the true Caliphs.

BELIEFS AND CULTURE

Muslims believe that there is one God, Allah, and that Muhammad was the last and greatest of his prophets. The Koran has many stories and traditions of the Old Testament, and in it are found stories of Adam, Noah, Abraham, Moses and David. Even Jesus Christ is mentioned in the Koran, although he is regarded as a prophet and not the Son of God. The word 'Muslim' means one who submits and anyone who can truthfully say 'There is no God but Allah: Muhammad is his messenger', is a Muslim.

Islam is based on five great beliefs which are laid down in the Koran. They are called the Five Pillars of Islam. They are:—
1 *Statement of belief.* Muhammad insisted that there was only one God, Allah, and that he, Muhammad, was his prophet. Muslims recite this creed daily.
2 *Prayer five times a day.* Prayer must be said five times a day: at dawn, just after noon, before sunset, just after sunset and during the early part of the night. Prayers can be said anywhere because the whole world belongs to Allah. The Friday noon prayers should be said in a Mosque, if possible, where an Imam or leader will lead the worship. Before praying, a Muslim always washes his face, hands and feet. Prayers are always said facing towards Mecca.
3 *Money to help people.* A true Muslim must always help wherever he can. He is expected to give money in the form of a tax known as Zakat.
4 *Keep the Fast of Ramadan.* During the month of Ramadan God first spoke to Muhammad and to mark this month true Muslims do not eat or drink between sunrise and sunset. Once the sun has set, one can eat. At the end of Ramadan there is a big festival called Id which is a feast of great fun and merrymaking.
5 *Pilgrimage.* Once in his life-time every Muslim should make a pilgrimage, the 'hajj' to Mecca, the Holy City during a special month. Some Muslims have to save all their lives to make this one journey. When they arrive at Mecca they have to go round the Kaaba seven times and then kiss the Black Stone. After making the pilgrimage a Muslim may call himself Hajji. After the pilgrimage most Muslims go to the City of Medina where Muhammad spent much of his life and where he is buried.

Muhammad always spoke against the keeping of idols and for this reason there was very little painting done. Instead, great attention was paid to beautiful lettering, and phrases from the Koran were carved in wood, stone and gold. It was also laid down that prayers should be said in a clean place. One way of doing this was to lay down a prayer mat. This has led to the making of fine rugs and mats which has become a great art throughout the Muslim world.

Islam	Submission to the will of Allah. Often used to mean the lands where followers of Muhammad lived.	مصر
Muslims	The Believers. Those who have submitted to Allah.	Arabic script is read from right to left.
Hegira	The day of the flight of Muhammad from Mecca to Medina. The Muslim years start from this day, 622 A.D. We use A.D. Anno Domini—the year of Our Lord Jesus as the starting point for our dates. Muslims use A.H. Anno Hegira.	٣٥

The numerals here mean 35. |

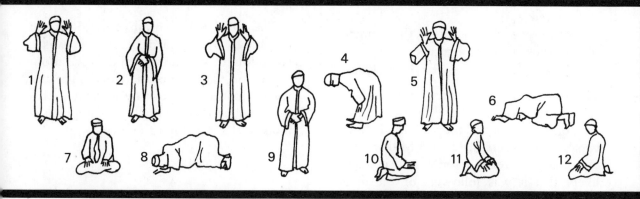

Prayer is one of the five pillars of Islam. Muslims pray five times a day. They pray in the direction of Mecca. Prayers can be said alone or in a mosque. The movements made by a Muslim during one sequence of prayer include raising their hands (1, 3 and 5), standing (2 and 9), bowing (4), lying face down in submission (6 and 8) and squatting (7, 10, 11 and 12).

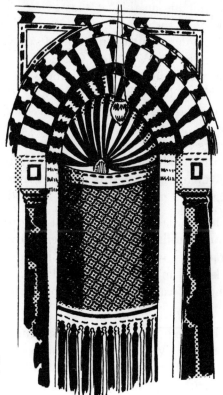

Every mosque has an alcove or niche called a mihrab. Facing the mihrab ensures the praying Muslim that he is facing towards Mecca.

47

Islam

THE KORAN

In the name of Allah, the Beneficent, the
  Merciful.
Praise be to Allah, Lord of the Worlds,
The Beneficent, the Merciful,
Ruler of the Day of Judgement.
Thee alone we worship; Thee alone we ask
  for help.
Show us the straight path,
The path of those whom thou hast
  favoured;
Not of those who have earned thine anger,
Nor of those who go astray.

The Koran

This is from the first chapter, or Sura as it is
called, of the Koran. There are one hundred
and fourteen suras and they are divided into
verses. It is not certain whether Muhammad
was unable to read or write, and it seems
likely that it was followers of the great
prophet who wrote down what he said. It
was after his death that the sayings were
made into the Koran. The Koran holds
those sayings which Muhammad said were
dictated by the Archangel Gabriel from the
great book in heaven. This divine work was
started by Muhammad about AD 610 in
Mecca, and was continued until his death in
Medina in AD 632. Muhammad's own
sayings are collected in many books called
Hadith (Traditions). Muslims revere them
as Muhammad's words, they revere the
Koran even more as the Word of God.

The Word of God has a special place in the
life of a Muslim. Muslim children know the
Koran very well indeed for it is the chief
book used in school and no day goes by
without a reading and recitation from the
great work.

The Koran, like the Old Testament, does
not only give a Muslim instruction in
spiritual affairs, it governs his whole life. It
deals with the laws of marriage and divorce,
says how goods are to be shared when a
person dies, describes the duties of parents
and employees. In business life no contract
is completed unless part of the Koran has
been recited.

Many of the Jewish and Christian
prophets are also prophets of Islam, and it is
natural, therefore, that some of the stories
of the Koran are the same as those in the
Jewish-Christian Bible.

The word Koran means recitation, and
the book is so called because it was a
recitation by Muhammad of the revelations
from God. It is one of the world's greatest
works. In its framework are all the rules that
made a nation turn from the worshipping of
idols to the worship of one God.

*This Koran was written in Morocco in 1568
A.D. The Koran is the holy book of the
Muslims. It was given by Allah to Muhammad
through the Angel Gabriel.*

The Call to Prayer.
Allahu akbar!
Allahu akbar!
Allahu akbar!
Allahu akbar!
Ashhadu an la ilaha illa-llah!
Ashhadu an la ilaha illa-llah!
Ashhadu anna Muhammadan
    rasulu-llah!
Ashhadu anna Muhammadan
    rasulu-llah!
Hayya ala s-salat!
Hayya ala s-salat!
Hayya ala l-falah!
Hayya ala l-falah!
Allahu akbar!
La ilaha illa-llah!

God is most great!
God is most great!
God is most great!
God is most great!
I testify that there is no God
    but God!
I testify that there is no God
    but God!
I testify that Muhammad is the
    Apostle of God!
I testify that Muhammad is the
    Apostle of God!
Come to prayer!
Come to prayer!
Come to salvation!
Come to salvation!
God is most great!
There is no God but God!

Each Nation has given the mosque its own national characteristic.

Tunisia

Pakistan

Egypt

Turkey

Indonesia

China

Great Britain

49

Hinduism

EARLY HISTORY

When the Aryan invaders first conquered northern India before 1200 BC, they brought with them a religion that was similar to that of the ancient Greeks and Romans. Some of the words used by the Hindus are almost the same as those used by the Greeks and Romans. For example, God in Latin is 'deus' and in Sanskrit (the language of the Hindus) it is 'deva'. When the Aryans arrived, they brought with them their own sacred books, the Vedas. These date back to before 1000 BC and are some of the oldest writings that exist today. Their religion, sometimes called Vedic religion, was closely connected with the power of nature. Sacrifices to various gods were common. Two of these gods, Shiva and Vishnu, became important later.

As time went by, this early religion changed. Other sacred books, such as the Upanishads, were written. The caste system which grew in strength divided the people into four main groups: the Brahmins or priests; the Kshatriyas or warriors; the Vaishyas or farmers and merchants; and the Shudras or servants. There came a time when wise Brahmins began to realise that their Vedic gods were poetic aspects of one supreme God, a reality they called Brahman. To know Brahman, God, inwardly became important. They also felt that one life was not enough. We need many lives to come to a knowledge of Brahman. Deep thought and prayer, in other words yoga, was now stressed.

THE EPICS

About the time of Christ, two great Indian poems were written, the Mahabharata and the Ramayana. The Mahabharata is the longest epic poem ever written. Part of it, called the Bhagavad Gita, gives many of the beliefs on which Hinduism is based. It explains that the soul or self is more important than the body. Death cannot harm the soul. The Bhagavad Gita stresses the caste system. It says that the whole world is part of Brahman, God. Brahman can take many forms. One of them is Krishna. The Bhagavad Gita is the 'Song of Krishna'. In it he says: 'Think of me, have faith in me, adore and worship me'.

In the Ramayana, Rama is the key person. Every autumn, in Indian villages and towns, Hindus act the story of Rama for two weeks. Rama's father, the king, appointed Rama to succeed him. There was joy among the people. But Rama was cheated of his throne and he was exiled to the forest. His faithful wife Sita, and his loving brother Lakshmana, went with him. In the forest they began to suffer. Sita was stolen by a demon king and taken to Lanka. Rama went after her and fought a great battle. The good Rama defeated the evil demon king Ravana. He took Sita back home where he became king and she became queen in an ideal kingdom that Indians call Ramarajya, the kingdom of Rama. Rama is the example Indians have of an ideal man, and Sita is the ideal woman. Their suffering and their kingdom have inspired Hindus down the ages.

The Veda			Other Hindu Holy Books	

The Vedas	Prayers and hymns
The Brahmanas	Duties of the priests
The Aranyakas	Religious teaching
The Upanishads	Brahman and the soul

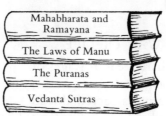

Mahabharata and Ramayana	Epic poems about Krishna and Rama
The Laws of Manu	How to live
The Puranas	Religious stories
Vedanta Sutras	Philosophical sayings

There are two kinds of Hindu holy books: the Veda–revealed from heaven; other holy books written and handed on by men. The Veda is more important although the Bhagavad Gita belongs to the second group. It is part of the Mahabharata.

The cow is a sacred animal. Gandhi said, "Cow protection is the gift of Hinduism to the world; and Hinduism will live as long as there are Hindus to protect the cow."

The great Hindu Temple at Madurai, Southern India.

Durgapuja–During this festival the goddess Durga is worshipped. Durga is an important goddess in Hinduism. She is a symbol of power.

51

Hinduism

STAGES AND WAY OF LIFE

The Hindu says that there are four stages of life. The first stage is being a student. At this stage Hindu boys receive a sacred thread which goes over one shoulder and around the body. This is worn at all times, night and day. The second stage is marriage and having a family. This is a Hindu's duty to society.

The third stage is when the family are grown up. A man and his wife can spend more time in thought and prayer.

At the fourth stage, some men leave their family altogether and walk the roads of India as holy men.

For Hindus there are four aims in life. The first is pleasure and enjoyment, kama. For a Hindu kama is part of religion. The second is making a living, or artha. Thirdly there is living the good life as far as one can. The word for this is dharma. The fourth aim is to gain release from rebirth and to find union with Brahman. This is the real goal of the Hindu, although he may be born many times before he reaches it.

The Bhagavad Gita mentions three ways of gaining release. One is the way of knowledge. It is not just knowing facts. It is knowing the meaning of life. The second way is that of devotion to a personal God. Love and trust in a personal God such as Vishnu, Shiva, Rama or Krishna can bring release. The third way is that of works. Gandhi said if you do your duty for its own sake, it can bring release. Work for God and others, without thinking about yourself, and you will find salvation.

HINDU BELIEFS

Brahman is the only true reality. Brahman is so great that it cannot be explained in human words, for humans are imperfect but Brahman is perfect. Hinduism teaches that only Brahman is real and that part of it is in everything.

Because Brahman is so far above the imagination of ordinary people, Hindus worship many gods who are stepping-stones to Brahman. Of all the gods three are very important. They are Brahma the creator, Shiva the destroyer, and Vishnu the preserver. Hindus believe that Vishnu has come down to earth in many forms. Two of these, Rama and Krishna, are much worshipped. Hindus are happy to say that God can be female and they are happy to worship a woman God.

Hindus believe that finally a person's soul, his Atman, will join with Brahman. When this happens there will be perfect happiness, and release from rebirth. This may not come about in one lifetime, because in most lives there are too many faults for this union to take place. What does happen is that the soul is never born and never dies, but only changes from body to body. Each change is decided by the life of the person in whom the soul has rested. If the deeds, the karma, of that person are good, then his next birth will be better. If the deeds of that person are bad, then his next birth will be worse.

Hindus believe that gods have heavens of their own. It is possible for a soul to stay for a time in the heaven of one of the gods before returning to earth. When someone dies in the holy city of Banaras by the river Ganges, he goes straight to Shiva's heaven. In Banaras there are two famous 'burning-ghats' where bodies of the dead are burnt. These ghats are steps down to the river on which there are logs to burn the bodies. However even going to heaven is not the end. One must be born again on earth in order to win final release and find union with Brahman.

The continent of India was divided in 1947 between the Muslim and Hindu religions. The Hindu regions became India. The Muslim regions became West Pakistan and East Pakistan. East Pakistan later became Bangla Desh.

Holy men, called sadhus, travel from place to place. The trident which some carry is a religious sign. All Hindus must give them food.

When a Hindu thinks he is about to die, he tries to visit Banaras. By bathing there in the river Ganges he will be freed from sin. The dead are dipped in the water, then burnt on a funeral pyre. The ashes are finally thrown in the river.

Hinduism

HINDU TEMPLES AND SERVICES

Hindu temples are often small, and they do not have set services. In the main part of the temple there is an image of a god. The priest of the temple receives offerings from worshippers who kneel one by one in front of the image. The priest often rings a bell to warn the god that a worshipper has come. The Brahmin priest usually says his prayers in Sanskrit, a language that many people do not understand. Most of the time, the priest looks after the image, washing, dressing and decorating it. The only part worshippers play is in giving the priest gifts and offerings for the god.

Festivals play an important part in the life of a Hindu. At these times an image is made out of bamboo, hay and mud from a sacred stream. A priest performs a ceremony so that a god will live in the image, and the image is now sacred. At the end of the festival the image is taken to the river and dropped in the water. It is sacred only during the festival. Often several villages join together for such a festival and much of the time is spent in dancing, plays and music.

There are many festivals because there are many gods. Most of them have feast days. The birthdays of the important gods such as Shiva, Rama and Krishna are very special. On these days the great temples are crowded. Inside and outside the temples are what we would call Fairs.

Most Hindus worship at home at sunrise, midday, and sunset. They do not have to go to a temple. Once a year, Hindus remember their fore-fathers in a special ceremony. This service is led by the eldest son of the family. It is important for a Hindu that there should always be a son to lead this service. One room in the house is set aside for family worship. It is used for nothing else and is very special. In this room will take place the four Hindu special services to do with birth, receiving the sacred thread, marriage, and death.

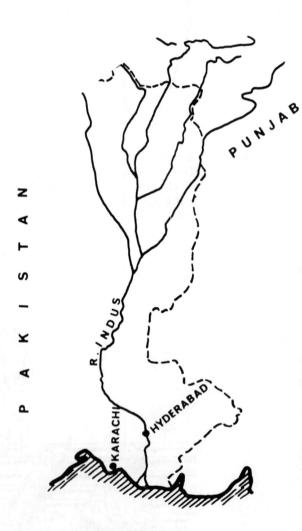

The word Hindu comes from the Persian word 'hind', the name for the region across the Indus River in N. India.

SHIVA–the destroyer. Hindus who worship Shiva are interested in learning and self-control. They believe new things can come only if the old are destroyed.

BRAHMA–the creator. The four heads show that Brahma has a mind that thinks on all things.

VISHNU–the god of love. Followers of Vishnu believe he has been to earth several times. These drawings show three of the forms he took: a tortoise, a fish, and a boar. Vishnu also came to earth in other forms including Rama and Krishna.

Hinduism

THREE MODERN HINDU REFORMERS

Like other religions, Hinduism has changed in the modern world. Hindu reformers have tried to bring it up to date.

Ramakrishna lived from 1836 to 1886. He was a man of deep prayer. His main love was for the goddess Kali and he lived in Calcutta which takes its name from Kali. Ramakrishna had visions of Kali and other Hindu gods as well as the gods of other religions. He was a man of deep religious experience.

There is an Indian story about five blind men. One day they came near an elephant. One man felt the leg of the elephant, another felt its trunk, another felt its tail, another felt its ear, and another felt its side. Each one thought they knew what an elephant was, but they did not. They knew what part of an elephant was. According to Ramakrishna, it is the same with religion. All religions have part of the truth, none of them have all the truth. Modern Hinduism believes this and the Ramakrishna Mission (named after Ramakrishna) teaches it.

Radhakrishnan was a great philosopher who became the President of India. He pointed out that old Hindu beliefs are still true — Brahman, rebirth, the soul etc. — but Hindus must pass them on in words that people can understand today.

A third reformer was Mahatma Gandhi. He was born in 1869, and is famous for his work in politics. It was largely due to him that India became a free country. Ramakrishna's way had been the love of God, President Radhakrishnan's way had been the knowledge of God, Gandhi's way was to work for God. He worked for the poor, he worked for social reform, he lived in a simple way. He said that is was wrong to use force, even against your enemies. He

went to prison more than once for opposing the British who then ruled India. In the end, India became free. By his example, Gandhi had shown Hinduism in action.

The caste system was brought to India about 1000 B.C. by the Aryan invaders from Northern Persia. It gradually became a part of the Hindu religion.

काकौ वृक्षे वसत:

The Hindu scriptures are written in Sanskrit. This means: "Two crows dwell in a tree".

Hindus are divided into four main castes.

BRAHMINS
(priests)

KSHATRIYAS
(warriors and rulers)

VAISHYAS
(workers and merchants)

SHUDRAS
(unskilled labourers)

OUTCASTES *belong to no caste. They do the lowest tasks*

Sikh Religion

The word Sikh means disciple. The first Sikhs were the disciples of the Teacher or Guru Nanak.

THE GURUS

Guru Nanak, a Hindu, was born near Lahore in the north-west of India in 1469. At this time mainly Hindus lived in the north-west part of India but they were ruled by Muslim emperors. Guru Nanak taught that the two peoples could live together in peace. He travelled far and wide over India teaching that there was one God and under God all men were brothers. He died in 1538.

The second Guru Angad built temples, Gurdwaras, where the Sikhs met.

The emperor Akbar granted to Ram Das, the fourth Guru, a piece of land. On the land the Guru had a large lake made in the middle of which was an island. On this island the fifth Guru Arjan (1563-1606) built a Gurdwara. The lake was called Amrita Saras, or Pool of Nectar. Around the lake and the temple grew the town of Amritsar. Amritsar is now one of the largest towns in the north-west part of India.

The emperor Jahangir had Arjan tortured and executed at Lahore. The death of their Guru turned many Sikhs from peaceful ways to fighting for their faith.

It was the tenth Guru Gobind Singh who turned them into warriors. This happened in a dramatic way. At a great meeting in 1699 Guru Gobind Singh appeared sword in hand and asked if there was anybody who was willing to die for his faith. Five men stood up and they were taken into a tent. Five times there was a sound of sword swishing and a stream of blood came from under the tent. Other men stood up and volunteered to die for their faith. Guru Gobind Singh came out of the tent followed by the five men dressed in yellow uniforms with bright swords at their side. The Guru embraced each one and called him 'my beloved Singh', which means lion.

They were given the name Khalsa, the pure ones. During that week over eight thousand people were baptised and became members of the Khalsa. They took the name Singh and were entitled to the five Ks.

THE FIVE Ks

The Five Ks Guru Gobind Singh gave his brotherhood were:—

Kesh — long hair on the head and chin. A Sikh never cuts his hair. The hair on the head is knotted in a special way and covered with a turban. (The long hair is part of the faith of a Sikh, the turban is a dress custom.)

Kangha — a comb for the hair.

Kach — short knee-length trousers.

Kara — a steel bracelet originally to protect the wrist from the bowstring.

Kirpan — a short steel sword.

Not all Sikhs became members of the Khalsa. Sikhs who are not members of the Khalsa do not have to grow a beard.

The Five K's

1. *Kesh*

2. *Kangha*

3. *Kach*

4. *Kara*

5. *Kirpan*

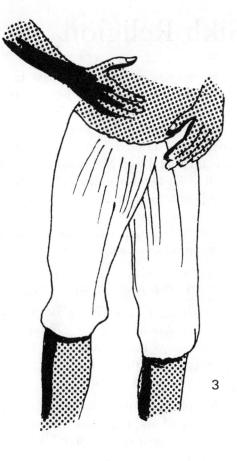

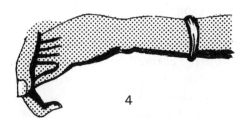

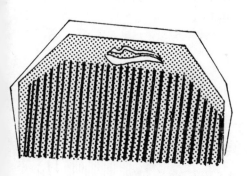

Sikh Religion

The home of the Sikhs is in the north-west part of India where there are nearly twenty million. Many Sikhs have left their home state of the Punjab to live in Canada, the United States, East Africa, Burma, Hong Kong, Malaysia, and Britain. The five Ks are becoming less important among some Sikhs overseas. The Kirpan is often worn as a tie-pin, the Kach have become underpants. The Kara and Kangha are sometimes not worn at all.

BELIEF AND SCRIPTURE

The Sikh faith says 'There is one God, whom we should serve by leading a good life, obeying his commands. Pray by repeating the name of God'. There are no priests, no images or idols.

The holy book of the Sikhs is the Granth. The word means 'The Book'. It was started by the fifth Guru Arjan in 1602. It contains the hymns he and the other four Gurus wrote, plus some other Indian hymns. In 1705-6 the tenth Guru added some of his own hymns and those of the ninth Guru. He then said that there would be no more teachers, the Granth would take the place of the Gurus. It became known as the Guru Granth Sahib. The book is written in Punjabi and Hindi with some words from other eastern languages — Arabic, Persian, and Marathi. The theme of the Granth is the union of man's soul with God through good living and service to mankind.

WORSHIP

The Sikh church or temple is called a Gurdwara. It is a place where the homeless can sleep and the hungry can always get a meal. When people go to the Gurdwara, they wash their hands as they go in, and they take off their shoes before entering the prayer room.

The prayer room does not have seats. Everyone sits on the floor. This is to show that all people are equal before God. It teaches people to be humble.

The Guru Granth Sahib is placed on a cushion and covered with a cloth. There is a canopy above. The prayer leader starts the service. There is the singing of hymns and reading from the Guru Granth Sahib. The reading is done by any member chosen by the leader. As part of the service there is a talk. The service ends with prasad. In many British Gurdwaras this is semolina which has been cooked in butter over which sugary water has been poured. This has been blessed and is now passed round for everyone to eat.

After worship there is a meal for all. It is usually lentils and other vegetables with yoghurt and rice. This shared meal is a sign of equality.

CONFIRMATION

When a Sikh child is old enough to know what he is doing, he joins the Khalsa usually at the time of the festival Baisakhi. This is held in April on the birthday of Guru Gobind Singh.

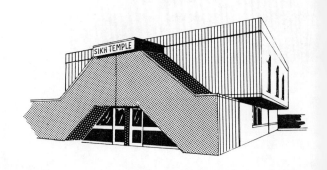

Sikh Gurdwara at Huddersfield

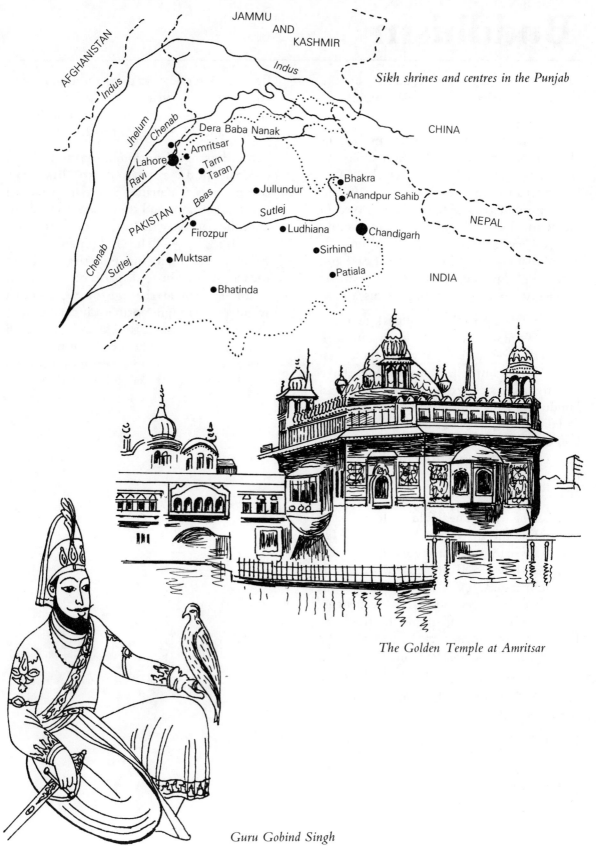

Sikh shrines and centres in the Punjab

The Golden Temple at Amritsar

Guru Gobind Singh

61

Buddhism

Three important parts of Buddhism are the Buddha, the Dharma, and the Sangha.

BUDDHA

The word, 'Buddha', is a title, and means 'The Enlightened One'. According to Buddhist tradition the title 'The Enlightened One' was given to an Indian prince, Siddhartha Gautama, who lived in Northern India about 600 years before Christ. He was the son of a wealthy Rajah. It is said that Gautama lived a life of ease and luxury in his palace, and for many years he never saw poverty, suffering or disease.

While driving to the royal park he came upon a wrinkled old man, a loathsome sick man and a dead man. The sight of these men made him ask himself: 'Why do people have to suffer pain, sickness and death?' He was a Hindu and believed that people, after they had died, came back to earth to live another life. Gautama thought about the problem of how one could escape from this everlasting round of suffering, dying and coming back again to earth to suffer and die once more.

When he was 29, he left his wife and baby son to find the answer to this problem. He cut off his hair, put on a yellow robe, took a begging bowl and joined two famous Brahmin monks. After two years with them, he felt he was no nearer the answer. Then, with five companions, he tried, by fasting, to find an answer. For six years he lived on little food, but he found that fasting only weakened his body and his mind.

Prince Gautama left his companions, but before he had gone far, he fainted. Nanda, a herdsman's daughter, found him, cradled his head on her lap and fed him with rice gruel until he was able to crawl to a hut. There she looked after him, feeding him on rice and honey cakes until he was well enough to travel. He moved on to a place called Gaya. Here, he sat in the shade of a big fig tree. After 46 days of meditation he was enlightened — that is, he had found the answer to his problem in the four Noble Truths and the eight-fold path.

Siddhartha Gautama, having been enlightened, returned to his five companions at Banaras. There he preached his first sermon, and they were converted. Soon he had sixty disciples who called him The Buddha — The Enlightened One. Buddha sent them out into the world to preach the eight-fold path of salvation. Until he died at the age of 80, Buddha wandered through Northern India teaching the way of happiness. He did not teach about a God, for he believed that happiness comes through a man controlling his own mind, not through worshipping gods.

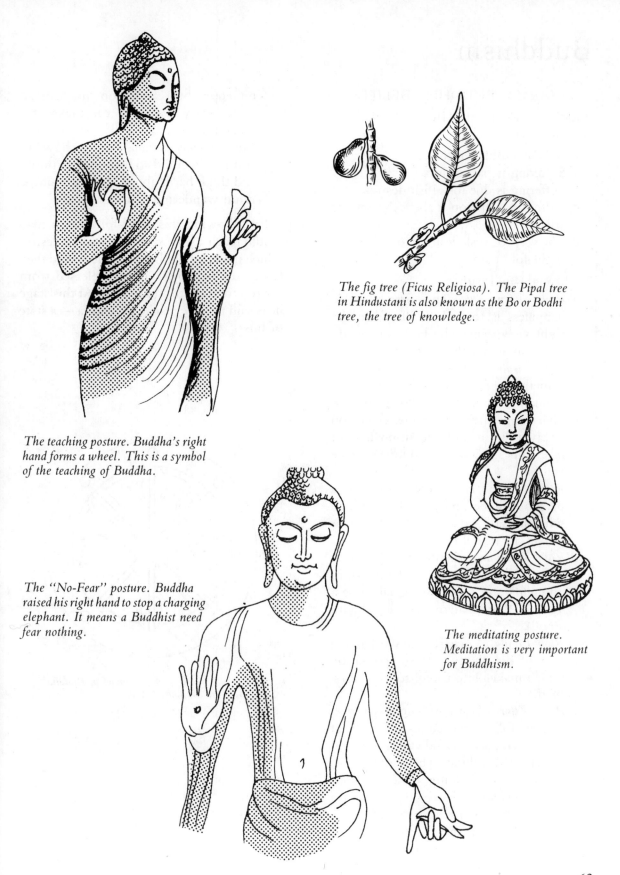

The fig tree (Ficus Religiosa). The Pipal tree in Hindustani is also known as the Bo or Bodhi tree, the tree of knowledge.

The teaching posture. Buddha's right hand forms a wheel. This is a symbol of the teaching of Buddha.

The "No-Fear" posture. Buddha raised his right hand to stop a charging elephant. It means a Buddhist need fear nothing.

The meditating posture. Meditation is very important for Buddhism.

Buddhism

DHARMA: BUDDHIST BELIEFS

Buddhists follow the Buddha's way of enlightenment.

1 The Four Noble Truths.
   a Suffering is part of life.
   b Suffering is due to selfish desires.
   c Suffering will stop if these desires are crushed.
   d The way to crush desire is to follow the eight-fold path.

2 The eight-fold path.
   a *Right Viewpoint.* The first step to happiness is to look at life from the right viewpoint. The best way to do this is to accept the four truths.
   b *Right Values.* Everyone hopes for something. The right way to go about obtaining the things we hope for is to give things their true value. A person always thinking of I, me, mine, has got false values. Kindness and love are true values.
   c *Right Speech.* Following this path, a person will be kindly and helpful in what he says, and will not boast or gossip, lie or tell tales.
   d *Right Behaviour.* Gautama taught that right behaviour comes from right thoughts and from loving all things. He said: 'Let a man overcome evil with good'.
   e *Right Living.* A man should work to the best of his ability, in an occupation which makes him useful to his fellow men.
   f *Right Effort.* Learn to know yourself and to follow the eight-fold path at your own pace. Avoid evil things and develop those things which give merit, such as love, thinking, concentration.
   g *Right Mindfulness.* Develop a calm and a freedom from unnecessary wants in the search for happiness. For example, wanting to eat does not make one unhappy, but eating too much or an unnecessary desire to eat makes for unhappiness.
   h *Right Contemplation.* Learn how to control the mind so that one can think, and think hard, about life, without the mind wandering to other things.

By following this eight-fold path a man would reach a state where he had no desires which made him unhappy — he would then reach true happiness and be released from the round of death and rebirth. At this stage he is said to have reached Nirvana — a state of bliss.

The wheel of life and the wheel of Buddha's teaching. A symbol of Buddhism.

A boy is made a Buddhist.

He is dressed in rich clothes, for Buddha was once a prince.

He is dressed in rags with hair shaved, for Buddha gave up riches and became a holy man.

He is dressed as a monk. The boy then spends at least one night, sometimes as long as four months, in a monastery.

A Buddhist monk has no possessions except for his robe, a begging bowl for food, a razor for shaving and a filter to strain insects from his drinking water (see first commandment). The colour of the robe varies in different countries. In Burma it is yellow, in Tibet, red, in London, grey.

The Buddhist Commandments

For all Buddhists:
1. *Thou shalt not take life.*
2. *Thou shalt not take what is not given.*
3. *Thou shalt not be unchaste.*
4. *Thou shalt not lie.*
5. *Thou shalt not drink intoxicating liquors.*

For Monks:
6. *Thou shalt not be intemperate in eating and shall not eat after noon.*
7. *Thou shalt not engage in or witness singing, dancing or the acting of plays.*
8. *Thou shalt not use garlands, perfumes or ornaments.*
9. *Thou shalt not use high or luxurious beds.*
10. *Thou shalt not accept gifts of gold or silver.*

Buddhism

SANGHA: SPIRITUAL LIFE

In Buddhism monks take a leading role. The Sangha, the Buddhist 'Church', gives an important place to monks. They are essential to Buddhism. Buddhists value the spiritual life. Above all, they stress meditation. This is a form of prayer.

In order to meditate, one must lead a good life. This means being at peace with others. The Buddhists say that it is wrong to hurt other people. It is also wrong to hurt other living things in nature. This has made Buddhism the most peaceful of the world religions.

There are different ways of meditation. Buddha knew that people are different. He wanted people to meditate, each in their own particular way. In general the Buddhists stress two ways of meditation. The first way is to look at a particular thing, such as a circle of clay, some water, or a flame, and shut out everything else. This makes the mind calm and peaceful. The second way is to go deeper still. It is to seek for insight into the nature of things. It is to follow the Buddha in seeking enlightenment. It is to go beyond a calm mind to Nirvana itself.

THE SPREAD OF BUDDHISM

Buddhism spread across Northern India. In 270 BC King Asoka became Emperor of India. He was a strong Buddhist and sent missionaries to Ceylon and Burma, and these countries became Buddhist. According to Buddhist tradition in AD 60 the Emperor of China sent to India for missionaries. Two monks answered the call and went there. Later monks translated Buddhist holy books into Chinese, and Buddhism spread throughout the country. In the 2nd century AD Thailand became Buddhist. In the 6th century AD missionaries from China went to Japan where Buddhism quickly became, with Shinto, the chief religion.

In the first thousand years AD belief in Buddha was spreading throughout the countries of the Far East. In India it was dying. Emperors came to the throne who were more Hindu than Buddhist, and the Hindu faith gradually won back the people. Finally, Muslim warriers over-ran India and stamped out what was left of Buddhism. Since 1945 there has been a growth of interest in Buddhism in India. Today there are about five million in India and many more in the countries to the north and east.

THE SECTS OF BUDDHISM

There were many groups in early Buddhism. Two big groups remain today: Theravada, followed by the peoples of Sri Lanka, Burma and Thailand; and Mahayana followed by the peoples of Nepal, Tibet, China, Korea and Japan.

Inside a Buddhist temple (Burma).

The statue of Buddha.

A monk reading from a holy book. Candles, offerings of food and money, lotus buds in vases brought by the congregation.

The congregation, each with prayer mat, tea pot, bowl, betel nut box and spittoon. A service is also a social occasion for tea drinking and gossip.

Buddhism

Theravada Buddhists believe that Nirvana can be reached only by one's own right living; no one can help you, no God nor saint, one must do it on one's own. The road to Nirvana is a long road, but it can be reached by following the four precepts of Buddha. Travel along the road can be speeded up by acts of merit.

Mahayana Buddhists believe that there are Buddhas to whom one can pray for help in following the eight-fold path to Nirvana. For example, Pure Land Buddhists call upon Amitabha Buddha, the Buddha of Infinite Light, a merciful God who lives in the 'Pure Land' or the 'Great Western Paradise'. Through faith and devotion to Amitabha Buddha a man can enter Nirvana. Other Mahayana schools call upon other Buddhas. Mahayana Buddhists also call upon Bodhisattvas. These are Buddhist saints who have worked for many lives to gain Nirvana. When they are in a position to enjoy Nirvana, they give it up. Out of love for the world, they are born again into the world to help others achieve Nirvana.

Among the Mahayana Buddhists there is a big group known as Zen Buddhists. These people believe that to understand life one has to live it, not spend a long time reading, talking or thinking about it. One should live in moderation and kindness. There should be care and thought behind every action. Through the experience of life, one will suddenly come to an understanding of life, and with understanding, gain enlightenment.

THE BOOKS OF BUDDHISM

Some years after Buddha died, his disciples met to write down his sayings. They become part of the 'Bible' of the Theravada Buddhists which is known as the Tripitaka, the three baskets. About four hundred years after the death of Buddha, Mahayana Buddhists added other sayings to the Tripitaka. These sayings were called Sutras. To Mahayana Buddhists they are very important.

The great Temple at Budh Gaya.

The Bo tree is believed to be a descendant of the one under which Buddha sat.

Buddhist Temples and Holy places are built to symbolise the five elements.

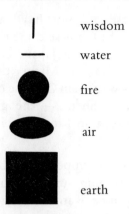

	wisdom
	water
	fire
	air
	earth

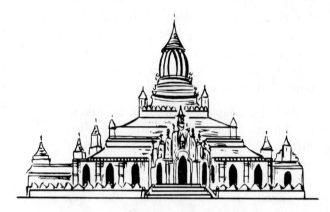

Pagoda (Burma)

Buddhist holy places have different names—each has its own national characteristic and each shows the elements from the broad base (earth) to the thin spire (wisdom).

Dagoba (Ceylon)

Pagoda (Japan, China)

Chotan (Tibet)

Chedi or Wat (Thailand)

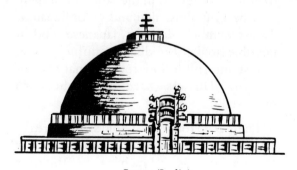

Stupa (India)

Shintoism

Shinto means 'The Way of the Gods' and is one of the religions of Japan. It is part of the Japanese way of life, and a Japanese simply cannot help joining in the national faith in some way or other.

As babies, Japanese children are taken to the Shinto shrine shortly after they are a month old to receive the blessing of the gods. They go to the shrine again at adolescence, on marriage, for special occasions: such as getting jobs, being promoted, reaching the age of 60 years.

In national life the Shinto rites of purification are performed for the launching of a ship, the consecration of a building, the opening of a bridge etc. The Emperor visits the chief shrine on his accession, cabinet ministers do so on their appointment, and royal messengers are sent to the shrine to tell the gods of events of national importance.

In many Japanese homes there is the 'Kamidanu', the god-shelf. On this shelf are tablets of clay or wood, or slips of paper. On these are written the names of the gods the family wish to honour. A small lamp burns on the shelf and the first rice cooked each day is placed there. The shelf is often decorated with twigs from the 'sakiki', the sacred tree of Shinto. At times during the day a glass of 'saki', wine made from rice, or 'mochi', rice cakes, may be put on the shelf to honour the gods. In the same room there may be a Buddhist altar and a Confucian or Taoist symbol, for the Japanese find it possible to be Buddhist, Confucian and Taoist and still follow the national faith of Shinto. This is hard for others to understand.

There is no founder of Shinto, as there is a founder of Buddhism or Islam, neither is there a holy book, such as the Bible or Koran, with directions from God on how to behave.

The Japanese did not have a written language until the Chinese came to Japan in the 5th century AD. The Japanese name for their religion, 'Kami no Michi' (the way of the gods), was written in Chinese characters as SHENTAO, 'Shen' — the gods, and 'Tao' — the way, as in Taoism. SHENTAO became SHINTO.

'Kami' means upper or above the ordinary. Anything unusual or which inspires awe can be 'Kami'. A large stone, a peculiarly bent twig, a mountain, a waterfall, a mighty chieftain, a learned scholar, thunder, lightning, the sun, these can all be 'Kami'. Hence, there are thousands of 'gods' in Shinto. Some of them are local to a tiny village and worshipped by a few villagers, others are national gods and worshipped by the whole nation. The religious tradition of climbing mountains is an interesting part of Shinto. The 'Kami' of Mount Fuji and Mount Ontake are very popular.

The Japanese characters for the word, Shinto.

A Tori is the symbol of Shinto.

A simple Tori.

Torii are built to mark holy places.

A more elaborate Tori.

*It is thought that the houses of the early Japanese
settlers were built in this style.*

Shintoism

In the 6th century AD Buddhist monks came to Japan, and Buddhism spread through the country. By the 8th century the Shinto priests were afraid that this new religion might drive out the old and that people would forget the old stories. They wrote some of the old legends of Shinto in two sacred books: the Kojiki — The Record of Ancient Events — and the Nihongi — The Records of Japan.

One of these legends was especially important. It tells how the sun goddess, Amaterasu, sent her grandson to rule over Japan. This meant that the emperor of Japan was divine, he was a descendent of the gods. This made the people of Japan revere their emperor, and it gave him great power.

According to the legend, Amaterasu gave her grandson three sacred objects with which to rule. They were jewels, the symbols of obedience and gentleness; a sword, the symbol of wisdom and justice; and a mirror, the symbol of goodness and purity. Jewels, a sword and a mirror remain the signs of the Japanese emperor who has been an important part of the Shinto religion.

SHINTO WORSHIP

A Shinto place of worship is called a shrine. Originally, a Shinto shrine was just a piece of ground marked out as holy. About the time of Christ it became the custom to erect simple wooden buildings as places of worship. They are usually small, for their purpose is not to be a place for people to meet but to be a house for the god. At the larger shrines there is a hall of worship in front of the smaller building, which is the home of the god. The two buildings are connected by a covered way.

In the house of the god, there is an emblem or symbol of the particular shrine. This emblem is known as the god-body, the 'Shintai'. It may be a hair, a strip of paper, a stone, a spear, or a sword. In the great national shrine of the sun goddess Amaterasu at Ise, the 'Shintai' is a mirror. Sometimes the 'Shintai' is an object of nature, such as a waterfall or a mountain.

Shinto holy ground is marked by a 'torii', a simple gateway of wood, stone or metal — two uprights sloping towards each other with two cross-pieces. It is thought that the word 'torii' means bird-perch. At many shrines the pathway from the 'torii' to the god-house is marked by 'toro', stone lanterns. The god-house may be guarded by Korean dogs, 'Komainu', sometimes known as 'Karashishi' or Chinese lions. Finally, there is the 'Gohei'. This is a small pole or wand of wood or bamboo from which hang strips of paper or of cloth folded into a plait design. The origin of the 'Gohei' is not known, but it is now recognised as a symbol of the gods.

The Jino stone.
A small stone put in a corner of the garden to honour Jino, the god who looks after property, has its own thatched roof shelter.

72

The Kamidanu, the god shelf.

A Japanese housewife offers the first rice of the day to the family's favourite god. On the Kamidanu is a tablet with the names of the god, the box containing the Shintai and two small stands for the daily offerings of rice and tea.

Grandmother offers tea to Daikoku and Ebisu, the gods of the kitchen.

A Shinto wedding procession.
The Shinto priest leads the procession, followed by the bridesmaids, bride and groom, fathers of the bride and groom, and friends. (Notice the mixture of traditional Japanese dress with western style dress.)

Shintoism

The shrines are looked after by the 'Kannushi', that is the 'Kami-nushi' or god-master. His job is to carry out the ceremonies according to the ritual, recite prayers and keep the shrine in good repair. He does not teach or preach and has no special training. He goes to work like other people, perhaps as a factory hand, farmer or fisherman. When doing his job as a god-master he wears special clothes.

At larger shrines there are often three groups of people. One group says the prayers at the rituals; another group, known as the purifiers, prepare the shrine and the offerings; the third group, called the diviners, declare the will of the gods by divination.

Most of the worship at a Shinto shrine is individual. The worshipper purifies his hands and his mouth at the trough of water and bowl of salt, goes to the front of the shrine, clasps his hands as a sign of respect, says his personal prayer and then leaves. A Japanese prays to his gods by giving thanks, not by reciting his sins and asking for forgiveness. An offering may be made. This the priest accepts with the correct ceremony.

FESTIVALS

Each village has its own local festivals to the local god, the 'Ujigami', the god of the village or the family. There are annual festivals to appease the gods who might destroy the harvests or destroy the fishing boats at sea. A great national festival of purification is held twice a year, on the last days of December and June. The ceremonies are led by the priests; the congregation take no part, they just watch. The priest moves round the shrine waving branches of the sacred sakaki tree and sprinkling salt, the symbol of purity.

The Japanese set great store on purity and being clean. They purify themselves after being in contact with dirt, disease, blood, earthquakes, accidents, stealing, lying, etc. They believe a pure heart is pleasing to the gods. To be pure and clean is part of the Shinto religion.

SHINTO AND JAPANESE RELIGION

It is wrong to think that Shinto is the only religion of Japan. The Chinese had talked about their 'three religions': Confucianism, Taoism, and Buddhism. When the Chinese came to Japan in the 6th century AD, they brought these three religions with them. In Japan they found a fourth religion, Shinto. Ever since these four religions have influenced each other. A Japanese may belong to all these four religions in different parts of his life. This is difficult to grasp in the West where a Christian cannot belong to another religion at the same time.

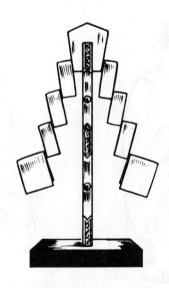

A Gohei. A Gohei, made of folded paper and bamboo, is the symbol of divinity.

The Sakaki, the holy tree.

Some Shinto sayings:–
*If in one's heart one is Kami, one
becomes Kami
If in one's heart one is a serpent, one
becomes a serpent.
It is evil
    that one should grow puffed up and
    should look down on others.
    that one should neglect his work in
    time of health.
    that one should fail to find daily
    occasion for gratitude.*

*The flowers are yellowish white and the berries
yellowish brown.*

*A mountain can be Kami. Mount Fujiyama, the holy
mountain of Japan, is the home of the goddess
Sengen-Sama.*

75

Shintoism

NEW RELIGIONS

In the last hundred years, and especially since the Second World War, over two hundred new religions have arisen in Japan. These new religions often include Shinto elements. They may also borrow from the other religions we have mentioned, as well as from Christianity which is now present in Japan.

The Second World War was a difficult time for Japan. At the end of the war the emperor announced Japan's defeat over the radio. He also told his people that he was not a god but only human. Some thought that Shinto would wither away because it had supported Japan during the war and it had stressed that the emperor was more than a man.

Shinto has not declined. It has grown stronger in itself and it has also helped the growth of some of the new religions. An example of a new Shinto sect is Tenri-kyo. It was founded in 1838 by a woman, Nakayama Miki. In some ways it is new. It calls itself a church, and stresses faith-healing. It is keen on social reform and it has many schools, libraries, hospitals, nurseries and clinics. It also sends missionaries to convert other people to Shinto so that people from outside Japan can now belong to Shinto. Its services may even include hymns, prayers and a sermon as in a Protestant church. In other ways it is old. Like ancient Shinto, it stresses purity and cleanliness. It says that evil and disease are due to eight dusts that fall on the soul. These dusts are greediness, meanness, undisciplined love, hatred, revenge, anger, pride and selfishness. The dusts must be cleansed from the soul by prayer, ritual and purification.

Yet it is not enough just to cleanse individuals. Tenri-kyo wants to cleanse the world as well. It works for a 'kingdom of peace' on earth. Shinto has its roots in Japan but through the work of these new Shinto groups it is becoming more of a world religion.

Toro. These are stone lanterns which lead from the tori to the shrine.

Inari, the rice god. Torii at his shrines are painted red. The fox is his messenger.

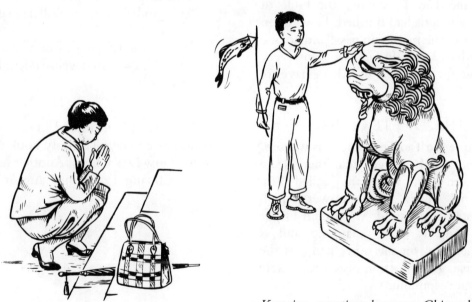

A Japanese woman prays at the steps of the shrine of the local god before going shopping.

Komainu, sometimes known as Chinese lions or Korean dogs, guard the shrine. The boy is wearing the suit in which he does gymnastics, and is carrying a paper fish for good luck.

Taoism and Confucianism

Legends tell us that Lao Tzu was born about 600 BC in the province of Honan in Central China. His name means the eldest or old master.

For most of his life Lao Tzu was an official at the court of a Chinese emperor, but he was not very happy there and finally he decided to leave and go westwards into the unknown parts of China. He left in a cart drawn by two black oxen. When he arrived at the last village before crossing the border into the unknown, he was recognised by a gatekeeper.

The gatekeeper knew Lao Tzu was a wise man who had great thoughts and he asked Lao Tzu to write down all those things which he thought were important. Lao Tzu spent several days writing down his thoughts and ideas. This writing was to become the Tao Te Ching, the bible of Taoism. When he had finished, he went on his way over the mountain pass, and no one ever saw him again. In fact, we know very little about the real Lao Tzu. All we have are legends.

THE TAO TE CHING

Long before the Tao Te Ching was written, the Chinese had believed that there were great unseen forces which they called 'Yin' and 'Yang'. Yang is the power which produces all firm, solid, warm and bright things. Yang is never changing and is masculine. Yin, on the other hand, is the power that gives soft, moist, changeable things and is feminine.

During the year sometimes Yang holds power (the summer months), and sometimes Yin (the winter months). In the same way, a person's life is governed by Yin and Yang. When everything goes well it is a period of Yang, when things go badly it is a period of Yin. In life the two powers must always be balanced. When this happens everything is perfect.

In the Tao Te Ching, it is taught that there is a Tao, or Way, which, if it is taken, will show how perfect balance in life can be reached. It is impossible to say exactly how to follow this path. A man has to find the path for himself. This is done by living simply and peaceably; by spending long hours in thought; by doing breathing and physical exercises; by being humble and thoughtful to fellow men. The Tao Te Ching tells us three great treasures which men can possess.

'I have Three Treasures. Guard them and keep them safe.
The First is Love.
The Second is Moderation.
The Third is never be first in the world.
With love, one will have courage.
With moderation, one will have power to spare.
Through not trying to be first in the world, one can develop talent and let it grow.'

The Tao Te Ching

Tao is pronounced Dow. Te is pronounced Day. The holy book is known as the Dow Day Ching. Another holy book is the Chuang Tzu named after its author.

According to legend Lao Tzu was born about 604 B.C. in the province of Honan. He was a recorder and librarian at the court of Chou, which probably accounted for his great knowledge of Chinese history. His great book, the Tao Te Ching, is very brief and has only just over five thousand words. It begins:—
    The Way (Tao) that can be spoken is not the Eternal Way. The Name that can be named is not the Eternal Name.

Ku-Sing

Ma-Chu

Kwan Ti

It was said that in China more gods were worshipped than there were people. In a Taoist temple provision is made for the worship of hundreds of gods. The three gods shown here are Ku-Sing, the god of literature; Ma-Chu the goddess of sailors and Kwan-Ti, the god of war.

The Chinese often have paper dragons at their festivals and use drums and fireworks. These are supposed to drive away evil spirits.

Taoism and Confucianism

LATER TAOISM

In later Taoism, there were two main groups. These groups were philosophical Taoism, and popular Taoism.

The philosophical Taoists followed the Tao Te Ching and the Chuang Tzu. Taoist thought had a big influence on Chinese painting, poetry, and music. Chinese painters and poets wanted to get close to nature. They wanted to get in tune with the Way, The Tao.

The second group was popular Taoism. It also used more popular ideas that appealed to the common people. Taoist priests went from village to village selling charms to bring good harvests and health, and magic drinks to give long life. They sometimes taught breath control, and they sometimes healed. They led services in the Taoist temples. Some of them became monks and spent more time in fasting and praying.

The Taoist church did not come into being until the second century AD and it was never well organised. Each local group tended to go its own way. Some even gave themselves fancy names such as The Taoist Red Eyebrows Society. This group led a rebellion against the government in AD 25. Another group, the Taoist Yellow Turban Society, led a rebellion in AD 184. The Taoist church was mainly popular religion. It spoke to the people at local level. It offered services, priests, gods, temples, and monks. In places it also offered magic, superstition, and peasant revolts. This seemed to be a long way from the ideas of the Tao Te Ching and Chuang Tzu.

The present Marxist government of China divides religion into two kinds.
Religion — Christianity, Islam, and Buddhism.
Superstition — Popular religions at the local level.

China now protects Religion but opposes Superstition. Taoism has been both. As a philosophy it has had a great influence on China. It still does. As a church, it is close to popular religion having elements of superstition. Because of this, it has declined. Though the Taoist church is weak, Taoist religious ideas have been central in the life of China.

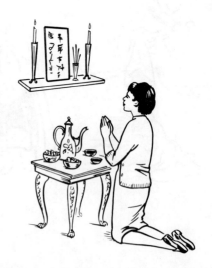

On the first and fifteenth of every month incense and candles are burnt before the god of the kitchen. Every year a sacrifice of meat is made and mock money burnt on the kitchen furnace. The Chinese believe that the kitchen god ascends to heaven and gives a report on how the family have behaved during the year.

In all Taoist temples the supreme god is shown as having three forms and existing as a divine trinity. The three gods are known as San-tsing, the Three Pure Ones. They are Yuh-hwang

Shang-ti, the creator and source of all truth; Wan-chang, who looks after learning; and Lao Tzu, who was made a god after his death.

During childhood a Taoist priest visits the house and sets up a paper door, an altar and images of gods.

The ceremony makes sick children better and keeps other children in good health.

Taoism and Confucianism

CONFUCIANISM

About 551 BC a boy was born into the K'ung family in the province of Shantung. The family was poor and the father died shortly after the baby was born. Despite this, the mother decided that her baby was going to have the best education that there was.

By the time he was fifteen the boy had decided that he would like to be a scholar and teacher. He studied very hard and learnt all he could of the history, poetry and music of Ancient China. He learnt that hundreds of years ago China had been a great united country. This made him think that if people could be brought back to the way of thinking that had existed hundreds of years ago, his country would again be great and united.

The teachings of the young man soon began to be known and he was eventually offered a high post in the state in which he lived. He made sure all his officials were honest and educated, and before long his government became famous. His fame made many people jealous and finally he had to leave his post.

K'ung went from state to state offering his services to princes, but nobody would listen to him. All the time he taught that it was possible to rule wisely and honestly. When he died in 479 BC few people knew of him. Many years later a record of his life and teachings, called the Analects, was written.

Missionaries first heard of him when they went to China, where he was called K'ung Fu-Tzu, which means 'Great Master K'ung'. Gradually, this was changed to Confucius.

HOW THE TEACHING OF CONFUCIUS BECAME A RELIGION

Confucius never thought of himself as a religious teacher, and whenever he mentioned religion it was to agree with ancestor and nature worship. He believed, that there was a Way of life, but he thought that this way was best reached by having rules for everyday living, rather than by leading a simple and bare life. Confucius was more interested in making rules on how people should behave to one another and conduct themselves in everyday life.

A change came about 200 BC, when a Chinese emperor went to the tomb of Confucius and offered sacrifices, and made the teachings of Confucius the way of conduct for all his officials. Later emperors honoured Confucius even more until, finally, he was almost given the status of a god.

CONFUCIAN CLASSICS

In the first century BC, five books called the Confucian Classics were made the basis for the Chinese examination system. For 2,000 years until our own century Chinese officials had to study these books and pass exams in them. Confucius had a very great influence on Chinese life in many ways.

The sayings of Confucius
Repay injury with justice and kindness. He who offends against Heaven has none to whom he can pray. Man is the representative of Heaven, and supreme above all things. There are five great evils. The man with a rebellious heart who becomes dangerous; the man who joins vicious deeds to a fierce temper; the man who is knowingly false; the man who treasures in his memory foul deeds and repeats them; the man who follows evil and spreads it.

Confucius is described in one of his writings as a man who in everything he did was an example to others. In his own village he was simple and sincere. Confucius believed that if a leader's example was good the people would also be good.

After the death of Confucius shrines were erected all over the empire honouring him as a wise man. Later he was given greater honour and almost raised to the status of a god. Prayers are not said at the shrines, but a Chinese kneels before them to show respect.

For hundreds of years before Confucius, ancestor worship had existed, and Confucius in his writings stressed that respect and devotion must be paid to ancestors.

Taoism and Confucianism

THE FIVE RELATIONSHIPS

The teaching of Confucius laid down the five great relationships. These relationships are:—

1 Ruler and Subject.
2 Father and Son.
3 Husband and Wife.
4 Elder and Younger Brother.
5 Friend and Friend.

Confucius laid down that peace and harmony and the 'Tao', or 'Way', could only be discovered if men knew of these relationships and carried out the responsibilities and duties which came from them.

Ruler and Subject. People in power should think of the welfare of their subjects. They should rule honestly and wisely. In return, the subjects must obey and carry out the wishes of the ruler.

Father and Son. The father must always show love to his son. He must clothe him, look after him and teach him. In return, the son must obey his father, look up to him and do as he is told.

Husband and Wife. A husband must always treat his wife properly and, in return, she must obey him.

Elder Brother and Younger Brother. The elder brother must be kind and helpful to his younger brother. He must guide him and help him. In return, the younger brother must be humble and show respect.

Friend and Friend. They should always act with honesty towards each other, and show one another respect.

Although the five relationships are the keystone of Confucianism, there are also many other rules by which men can live better lives. Several hundred years before Jesus gave the rule by which men should live, Confucius had written — 'Never do to others what you would not like them to do to you'.

Confucianism has had a great effect on the Chinese people. It has taught a way of life which has had an effect on the family, on the village and the town. Every man has had before him ideals up to which he should live, and the goals have been self-respect, generosity, sincerity and kindness.

CHINESE RELIGION

The two religions we have looked at balanced each other. Taoism stressed nature, being humble, and giving way to others. The Confucians stressed relationships, learning, and ruling others. These two religions are opposites, rather like Yin and Yang. They are female and male, soft and hard, cold and hot, black and white. But they belong together, they need each other. In the same way Taoism and Confucianism are opposites, but they need each other in the wider whole of Chinese Religion.

When the Buddhists entered China, Buddhism became the third way. The Chinese then talked about the three ways, the three religions. They were Taoism, Confucianism, and Buddhism. It was possible for a Chinese to belong to all three religions in different parts of his life. Chinese Religion was a mixture of all three.

This is the Temple of Heaven in Peking which is said to be the largest temple ever built for ancestor worship.

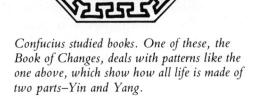

Confucius studied books. One of these, the Book of Changes, deals with patterns like the one above, which show how all life is made of two parts—Yin and Yang.

The Temple of Confucius was built about the 13th century and in it are tablets to commemorate Confucius and his disciples.

Baha'i Religion

The Baha'i religion is the newest of the religions in this book. It dates back only to 1844. It is new also in its ideas. It aims to bring together the people of the world and the religions of the world. It aims to make men and women equal. It aims to take seriously both science and religion. It speaks to the modern world as a modern religion. Although small in numbers, the Baha'is already have over 100,000 centres. They have spread, in small numbers, into most parts of the world.

HISTORY

Although the Baha'i tradition is named after Baha'u'llah, it goes back before him for its actual beginning. Its origins were in Iran where a small group of people were seeking a new religious leader for their age. Their search was ended when a young man who became known as the Bab (the Gate) said that he was the promised leader. He made this claim on 22nd May 1844 when he said 'I am the Bab, the Gate of God'.

He saw himself as the gateway to a new age of peace and of sharing among men and women. He also claimed, rather like John the Baptist in relation to Jesus, that a greater person than himself was about to come. After three years of preaching and three years in prison, he was put to death in 1850 by the leaders in Iran who were upset by the rapid growth of his movement.

Baha'u'llah was born in 1817. He had become a follower of the Bab. When an attempt was made to kill the Shah of Iran by two misguided followers of the Bab, Baha'u'llah was thrown into prison. In prison he had a great experience of the glory of God (that is what the word Baha'u'llah means). He now believed that he was the promised one of whom the Bab had spoken. The Baha'i religion proper therefore began in prison!

In 1863, at Ridvan, a garden near Baghdad, Baha'u'llah said that he was the promised one of all religions, that his message was for all mankind, and that a new time had begun in human history. He was sent into exile from one place to another until his death at Acre in 1892. By this time the Baha'i religion had spread into fifteen countries. Baha'u'llah had written personal letters about his work to many world rulers, including Queen Victoria who is said to have remarked 'If this is of God, it will endure; if not, no harm can come of it'.

Symbol of the greatest name, Baha. A Baha'i symbol

Baha'i archives building, Haifa

Baha'i House of Worship, Sydney, Australia

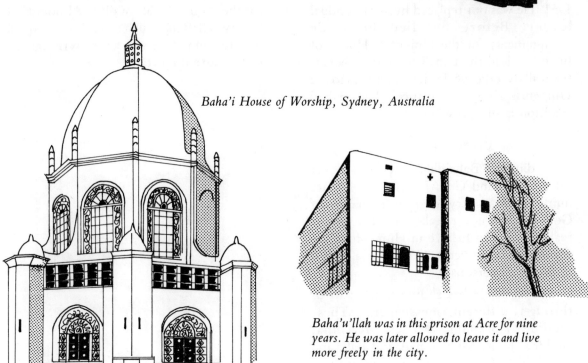

Baha'u'llah was in this prison at Acre for nine years. He was later allowed to leave it and live more freely in the city.

Baha'i Religion

The Baha'i tradition has endured. It has grown more after the death of Baha'u'llah than it did in his lifetime. Baha'u'llah's son, Abdul-Baha (the servant of Baha), continued his work and succeeded him as head of the movement. Abdul-Baha was a great leader, and a great writer. By the time he died in 1921, the Baha'i movement had spread to another twenty-three countries. Abdul-Baha had been born on that day in 1844 when the Bab had proclaimed himself the 'Gate of God' so his death at 77 marked the age of the Baha'i tradition itself.

Age gave way to youth. Abdul-Baha's grandson, Shoghi Effendi, was a 25 year-old student at Oxford when he followed his grandfather as 'Guardian of the Faith'. He too was a great leader and died in 1951. He was not replaced by an individual leader. Before he died he made arrangements for the Universal House of Justice to lead the Baha'i tradition. Baha'is from all over the world elect members to the Universal House of Justice. The Baha'i tradition is still growing.

VIEW OF GOD

According to Baha'u'llah, we can never fully understand God. He is God, we are humans. We can try to grasp the nature of God, we will never really succeed. God is real and we can believe in Him. He is the maker of the universe. He is also a loving father to all persons.

Above all He has shown himself to us through different messengers. These include Abraham, Moses, Krishna, Buddha, Jesus, Muhammad, the Bab, and Baha'u'llah. God has shown himself in all religions, in all religious messengers, and in all scriptures. Through them, we know much about God. Baha'is give to Baha'u'llah a special place among the messengers of God, but say at the same time that all religions point the same way in their spiritual teaching.

SACRED WRITINGS

The Baha'i tradition does not have one Holy Book such as the Bible or Koran. It has many sacred writings. These include the works of Baha'u'llah. Added to them, in practice, are the writings of Abdul-Baha and Shoghi Effendi. Although Baha'u'llah wrote more than a hundred works, some are read and used more than others. His main laws are found in 'The Most Holy Book' (al-Kitab al-Aqdas), his main teachings in 'The Books of Certitude', his main moral and spiritual thoughts in 'The Hidden Words', his mystical teaching in 'The Seven Valleys', and his last main work was 'Epistle to the Son of the Wolf'. Although, in theory, all Baha'u'llah's works are equally inspired; in practice the above writings tend to be more important.

The entrance to the shrine of Baha'u'llah, Bahji

Baha'i House of Worship, Frankfurt, West Germany

Baha'i Religion

WORSHIP AND COMMUNITY

The daily prayers said by all practising Baha'is are very important. The Baha'is have no priests, no sacraments, and little ritual. Their worship often takes place in houses, and it is in houses that many of their local 'spiritual assemblies' meet. These local assemblies are linked together by national assemblies that meet once a year. The national assemblies are linked together every five years by a great meeting of the Universal House of Justice at Haifa in Israel.

Every nineteen days, local Baha'is come together for a feast. This has three parts. One part is worship which includes the reading of some of the sacred writings, some prayers, and perhaps some music. Another part is the discussion of the business of the local community. The third part is the feast itself when there is eating and talking between Baha'i friends. Also important is a 19-day feast that takes place once a year when there is no eating or drinking between sunrise and sunset. In addition, there are nine holy days for the Baha'is. These include the birthdays of the Bab and Baha'u'llah, the days when the Bab and Baha'u'llah declared their mission to the world, and the days when the Bab and Baha'u'llah passed away from the earth.

All Baha'is give to the Baha'i Fund. Instead of a collection they give secretly as much as they feel they can afford. At present Baha'is think it is more important to spread their message than to use their money on costly buildings. However local houses of worship are planned for the future. Beautiful houses of worship have already been built or are being built in each continent. They are nine-sided, have fine domes and are open to all. On the same site are a school, a hospital, an orphanage, and a quiet place where people can rest and think.

ETHICS AND SOCIAL INVOLVEMENT

Baha'is feel that good morals are very important. They stress the simple virtues of purity, truth, and honesty. They do without drugs and alcohol. They avoid eating too much, and discourage smoking. Marriage and family life are an important part of the good life.

The Baha'is have also been very active in national and international matters. They have a deep concern for education, for giving women an equal role, for showing the importance of science in human life, for improving the quality of life. Above all they want to work for peace. They look forward to the peoples of the world joining together and working together for a better future. It is fitting that the Baha'i International Community is recognised by the United Nations. For they are clearly working for the unity of mankind that the United Nations also seeks. However they see that unity as including the spirit of man as well as his body and mind. They see that unity as including God.

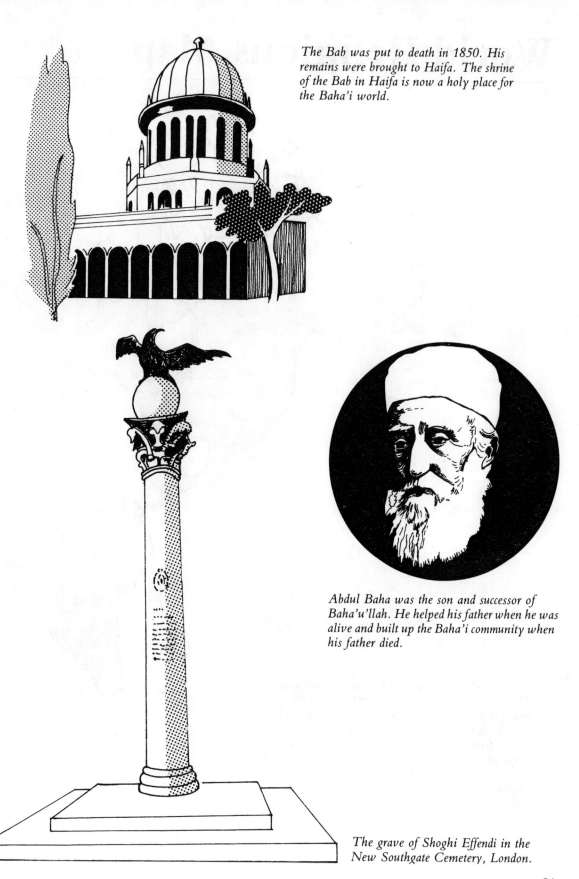

The Bab was put to death in 1850. His remains were brought to Haifa. The shrine of the Bab in Haifa is now a holy place for the Baha'i world.

Abdul Baha was the son and successor of Baha'u'llah. He helped his father when he was alive and built up the Baha'i community when his father died.

The grave of Shoghi Effendi in the New Southgate Cemetery, London.

World Religions Map

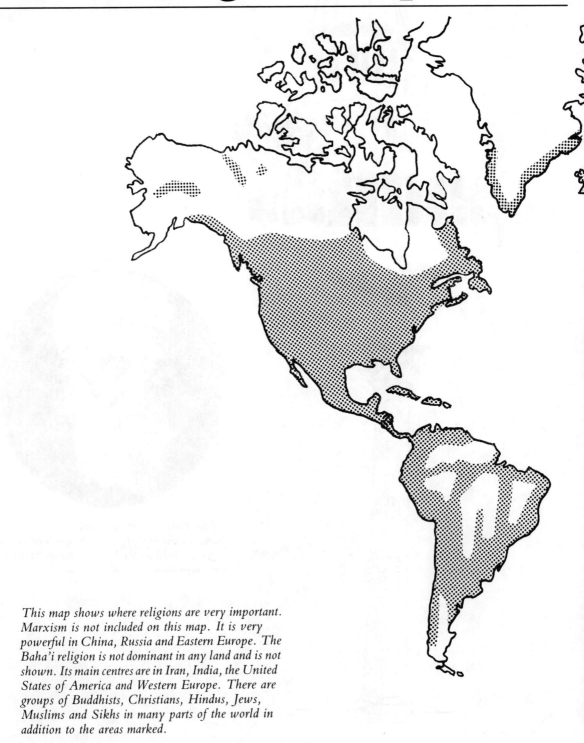

This map shows where religions are very important. Marxism is not included on this map. It is very powerful in China, Russia and Eastern Europe. The Baha'i religion is not dominant in any land and is not shown. Its main centres are in Iran, India, the United States of America and Western Europe. There are groups of Buddhists, Christians, Hindus, Jews, Muslims and Sikhs in many parts of the world in addition to the areas marked.

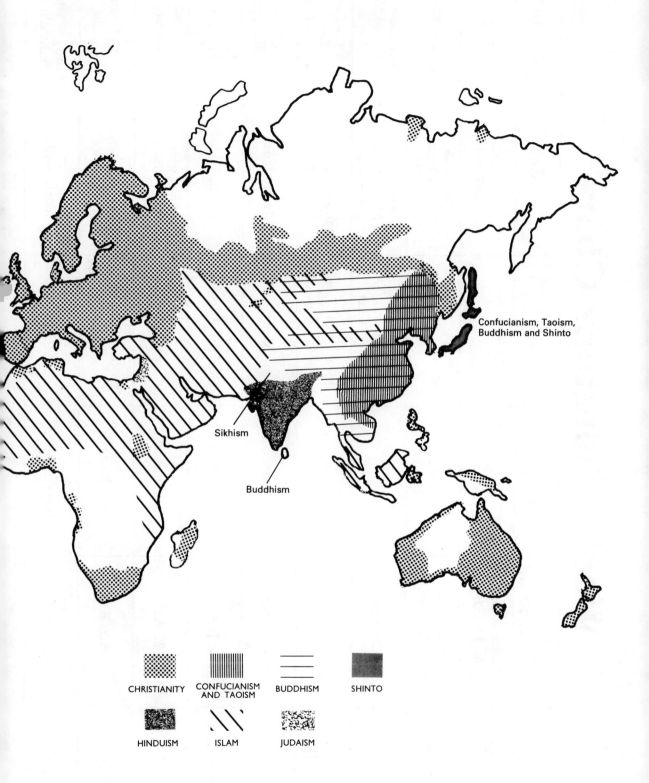

Confucianism, Taoism,
Buddhism and Shinto

Sikhism

Buddhism

CHRISTIANITY CONFUCIANISM BUDDHISM SHINTO
AND TAOISM

HINDUISM ISLAM JUDAISM

93

World Religions Chart

	DATE OF FOUNDING	FOUNDER	GOD	PLACES	HOLY BOOK
HINDUISM	Not known *(before 1500 BC)*	*None*	Brahman as Supreme Reality plus other gods	World wide Mainly India	Veda
JUDAISM	Not known *(before 1200 BC)*	Moses	Yahweh	World wide Mainly Israel and USA	Jewish Bible
BUDDHISM	Sixth Century BC	Gautama Buddha	No God: Nirvana transcendent. Some worship Buddha.	World wide Mainly South East Asia	Pali Canon or Tripitaka/Mahayana Sutras
CONFUCIANISM AND TAOISM	Sixth Century BC	Confucius *According to legend* Lao Tzu	Heaven or Tien The Tao	Mainly China and Far East	Five Confucian Classics Mainly Tao Te Ching
SHINTO	Not known	*None*	Many	Mainly Japan	Kojiki and Nihongi
CHRISTIANITY	4 BC	Jesus Christ	God the Trinity	World wide	The Bible
ISLAM	622 AD	Muhammad	Allah	World wide Mainly Africa to China	Koran
SIKHISM	c 1520 AD	Guru Nanak	God as Supreme Guru	Mainly Punjab but getting wider	Guru Granth Sahib
BAHA'I	1863 AD	Baha'u'llah	God	World wide	Mainly works of Baha'u'llah

Festivals Alluded to in this Book

1 January **Shinto New Year's Festival** *Ganjitsu*
18-25 January **Week of Prayer for Christian Unity**
17 February **Hindu Mahashivaratri** *Great Night of Shiva*
20 February **Ash Wednesday** beginning of Lent which ends 6 April
20 February **Birthday of Modern Hindu Saint Ramakrishna**
20 February **Chinese New Year** *Yuan Tan*
11 March **Chinese Full Moon Festival of Lanterns** *Teng Chieh*
31 March **Palm Sunday** *Jesus Rides into Jerusalem*
4 April **Maundy Thursday** *Last Supper of Jesus*
5 April **Good Friday** *Death of Jesus*
6-13 April **Jewish Passover** *Pesach* — recalling the Exodus out of Egypt
7 April **Easter Sunday** Resurrection of Jesus — 14 April in Orthodox Church
8 April **Buddha's Birthday** in Mahayana Buddhist Japan *Hanamatsuri*
13 April **Baisakhi** when Guru Gobind Singh founded the Sikh Khalsa
21 April to 2 May **Baha'i Festival of Ridvan** when Baha'u'llah declared himself the Promised One
End April **Rama Navami** Birthday of Hindu God Rama
13-18 May **Christian Aid Week**
16 May **Ascension Day** *Ascension of Christ*
20 May to 18 June **Muslim Fast of Ramadan**
23 May **Baha'i Anniversary of the Bab's Forecast of the Coming of Baha'u'llah**
26 May **Whitsun** *Coming of the Holy Spirit*
26-27 May **Jewish Pentecost** *Shavuoth* — recalling the giving of the Law at Mt Sinai
29 May **Anniversary of Death of Baha'u'llah** Baha'i
4 June **Vaisakha Puja** when Theravada Buddhists remember the birth, enlightenment and death of the Buddha
14 June **Lailat-al-Qadr** Muslim Night of Power when the revelations of the Koran began
19 June **Id-al-Fitr** Muslim celebration of the end of the Ramadan Fast
22 June **Chinese Dragon Boat Festival**
End June **Dhamma Vijaya** *Theravada Buddhist* Recalls first preaching of Buddhism outside India
9 July **Baha'i Anniversary of the Martyrdom of the Bab**
13-15 July **Obon** Shinto Festival welcoming back the spirits of the departed
End July **Asala** Theravada Buddhist Anniversary of Buddha's preaching of the Four Noble Truths at Banaras
End August **Janamashtami** Birthday of the Hindu God Krishna
16 Sept **Al Hijra** Muslim Anniversary of the Flight of Muhammad from Mecca to Medina
16-17 September **Rosh Hashanah** *Jewish New Year*
25 September **Ashura** Shiite Muslims recall the death of Husain, son of Ali
25 September **Yom Kippur** *Jewish Day of Atonement*
30 September to 8 October **Sukkoth** *Jewish Festival of Tabernacles*
21-28 October **Week of Prayer for World Peace** Many religions share in this
End October **Dassehra/Durgapuja** Hindu, recalls Rama's victory over Ravana and the Goddess Durga's victory over the demon buffalo
12 November **Birthday of Baha'u'llah** Baha'i
25 November **Birthday of Muhammad** Islam
End November **Birthday of Guru Nanak** Sikh
End November **Diwali** Hindu New Year's Festival of Lights
1 December **Advent** looks forward to the coming of Jesus at Christmas
25 December **Birthday of Jesus Christ — Christmas Day** 7 January in Othodox Church
31 December **Omisoka** Shinto Cleansing Festival
End December **Birthday of Guru Gobind Singh** Sikh
The dates here are those of 1985.
In some cases the exact dates are not shown because they are fixed in relation to the movements of the moon.

Index

Holmes McDougall, Edinburgh
0 7157 2355 3